Dialogical Engagement with the Mythopoetics of Currere

This volume showcases a series of chapters that elaborate on Mary Aswell Doll's contributions to the field of curriculum theory through her examination of *currere as a mythopoetics*.

By bringing Doll's Jungian, autobiographical, and literary perspectives into conversation with emergent forms of subjective inquiry—including aesthetic concepts, ecological questions, and spiritual themes—the volume foregrounds the originality and significance of Doll's book *The Mythopoetics of Currere* in particular, while simultaneously extending it and demonstrating its applications in various scholarly conversations. Leading scholars in the field of curriculum studies such as William F. Pinar and Molly Quinn demonstrate how they use Doll's ideas as pedagogy, as theoretical framing for their work, and as the basis of their own study and self-exploration. A response essay from Doll herself concludes the text, bringing further thought and insight to the mythopoetic dimensions of *currere*.

This text will benefit scholars, academics, and students in the fields of curriculum studies, curriculum theory, and the foundations of education more broadly. Teachers and teacher educators interested in the conceptualization of curriculum in humanities education will also benefit from this volume.

Brian Casemore is Associate Professor of Curriculum and Pedagogy in the Graduate School of Education and Human Development at The George Washington University, Washington, DC, USA.

T0323165

Studies in Curriculum Theory Series
Series Editor: William F. Pinar, University of British Columbia, Canada

In this age of multimedia information overload, scholars and students may not be able to keep up with the proliferation of different topical, trendy book series in the field of curriculum theory. It will be a relief to know that one publisher offers a balanced, solid, forward-looking series devoted to significant and enduring scholarship, as opposed to a narrow range of topics or a single approach or point of view. This series is conceived as the series busy scholars and students can trust and depend on to deliver important scholarship in the various "discourses" that comprise the increasingly complex field of curriculum theory.

The range of the series is both broad (all of curriculum theory) and limited (only important, lasting scholarship)—including but not confined to historical, philosophical, critical, multicultural, feminist, comparative, international, aesthetic, and spiritual topics and approaches. Books in this series are intended for scholars and for students at the doctoral and, in some cases, master's levels.

A Praxis of Presence in Curriculum Theory
Advancing *Currere* against Cultural Crises in Education
William F. Pinar

The Nordic Education Model in Context
Historical Developments and Current Renegotiations
Edited by Daniel Tröhler, Bernadette Hörmann, Sverre Tveit, and Inga Bostadt

Parental Experiences of Unschooling
Navigating Curriculum as Learning-through-Living
Khara Schonfeld-Karan

For more information about this series, please visit: https://www.routledge.com/Studies-in-Curriculum-Theory-Series/book-series/LEASCTS

Dialogical Engagement with the Mythopoetics of Currere

Extending the Work of Mary Aswell Doll across Theory, Literature, and Autobiography

Edited by Brian Casemore

Routledge
Taylor & Francis Group

NEW YORK AND LONDON

First published 2022
by Routledge
605 Third Avenue, New York, NY 10158

and by Routledge
4 Park Square, Milton Park, Abingdon, Oxon, OX14 4RN

Routledge is an imprint of the Taylor & Francis Group, an informa business

Library of Congress Cataloging-in-Publication Data
Names: Casemore, Brian, editor.
Title: Dialogical engagement with The mythopoetics of currere : extending the work of Mary Aswell Doll across theory, literature, and autobiography / edited by Brian Casemore.
Description: New York, NY : Routledge, 2022. | Series: Studies in curriculum theory | Includes bibliographical references and index.
Identifiers: LCCN 2022003749 | ISBN 9781032139296 (hardback) | ISBN 9781032139319 (paperback) | ISBN 9781003231547 (ebook)
Subjects: LCSH: Education—Curricula—Philosophy. | Education—Biographical methods. | Reflective learning. | Doll, Mary Aswell. Mythopoetis of currere.
Classification: LCC LB1570 .D53 2022 | DDC 375—dc23/eng/20220302
LC record available at https://lccn.loc.gov/2022003749

ISBN: 9781032139296 (hbk)
ISBN: 9781032139319 (pbk)
ISBN: 9781003231547 (ebk)

DOI: 10.4324/9781003231547

Typeset in Times New Roman
by Apex CoVantage, LLC

Contents

About the Editor and Contributors

Brian Casemore is Associate Professor of Curriculum and Pedagogy at The George Washington University in Washington, DC, USA.

Mary Aswell Doll is Professor Emerita of English in the Liberal Arts Department at Savannah College of Art and Design, Savannah, Georgia, USA.

Marilyn Hillarious has worked as Adjunct Faculty in the Department of Curriculum and Pedagogy at The George Washington University in Washington, DC, and in the Department of Curriculum, Instruction and Special Education at the University of Virginia in Charlottesville, Virginia, USA.

William F. Pinar is Tetsuo Aoki Professor in Curriculum Studies at the University of British Columbia, Vancouver, Canada.

Molly Quinn is an Endowed Professor and Director of the Curriculum Theory Project at Louisiana State University, Baton Rouge, Louisiana, USA.

Introduction

On the Expressive Forms and Dialogical Depths of Mythopoetic Curriculum

Brian Casemore

> "We are not removed from that which we study, for we study in order to know ourselves and to reach out to the public sphere."
>
> (Doll, 2017, p. 142)

This collection of essays explores and expands the significance of Mary Aswell Doll's scholarship in the field of curriculum studies by dialogically engaging her book *The Mythopoetics of Currere: Memories, Dreams, and Literary Texts as Teaching Avenues to Self-Study*. Doll's unique approach to *currere*—curriculum as lived experience—emerges from her understanding of the self as layered fictions of personal, social, and historical origin and, therefore, as available to be interpreted and revivified through engagements with fictive, poetic, and cultural texts. The study of *currere*, inaugurated and conceptualized by William Pinar (1975/1994, 2012), provides the foundation for Doll's mythopoetic curriculum project. Doll undertakes "the running of the course" (Pinar, 2012, p. 44) with a literary orientation that vitalizes the text of human experience: the shadows and kaleidoscopic manifestations of psychic life made legible for study, translation, and contextualization. The authors of *Dialogical Engagement with the Mythopoetics of Currere* pursue various threads of Doll's work to elucidate her study of *currere* in a mythopoetic register. In her book, Doll interweaves autobiography born of dreaming and deep remembrance, critical and imaginative literary analysis, close readings of depth psychology and curriculum theory, and pedagogical reflections on the inner dimensions of humanities education. Entering this rich nexus of thought, the authors of the collection explore curriculum as a subjectively interior process symbolized in worldly form. They consider *The Mythopoetics of Currere* in terms of its threading of meaning, theory of inscape, ethics of relationality and listening, and embodiment of spirit and soul. Responding to the first four chapters in the collection, Doll herself furthers the conversation.

DOI: 10.4324/9781003231547-1

By way of introduction to the book, I share a memory of an early encounter with Mary—the story of a conversation about literature and its dialogical extension. I proceed autobiographically in the spirit of Mary's work to characterize the dialogical depth that imbues her scholarship and the essays in this collection.

During the second year of my doctoral studies, in December 1999, I attended a holiday party at Bill Pinar and Jeff Turner's home in Baton Rouge, Louisiana, where I had one of my first conversations with Mary. I spoke with her about my emerging research interests and mentioned that I was completing a course on "the literature of memory" taught by the prominent scholar of autobiography James Olney. Having read a few of Mary's essays in curriculum theory—specifically, "Beyond the Window: Dreams and Learning" (Doll, 1982/1999) and "Winging It" (Doll, 1997)—I had a sense of her extraordinary study and teaching of literature, and I was eager to demonstrate that we were co-journeyers[1] in literary education—that I too grasped the literary work as the "angel in the classroom" (Doll, 1997, p. 5), "whose wings release desire and awe" (p. 4). In the conversation, Mary listened most generously to my earliest efforts to understand literature as curriculum that demands autobiographical labor, and she spoke of literature—fictive, mythic, and lyrical—with an ebullience and subtlety that expressed the depth of a life forged through such reading. This encounter with Mary, its significance threading outward in my experience of study and teaching, I now realize, engendered in me a sense of curriculum as an imaginative literary text that enfolds subjectivity and discloses the complexity of self-formation.

As Mary and I talked, we wandered around some of our most beloved literary worlds. Enlivened by the sense of literary fellowship, I shared with some excitement my experience of James Olney's course, elaborating on his remarkable syllabus,[2] one that charted the study of memory in states of animation, trouble, loss, and recovery. In that course, among other wonderful texts, I explained, we read Saint Augustine's *Confessions*, Eudora Welty's *One Writer's Beginnings*, Virginia Woolf's *Sketches of the Past*, Jorge Luis Borges' "Funes the Memorious," Gertrude Stein's *The Autobiography of Alice B. Toklas*, and Samuel Beckett's *Krapp's Last Tape*. Mary expressed delight about it all, but it was Woolf and Beckett—literary inspirations she finds supremely rousing and provocative—who led us into deeper conversation: Virginia Woolf, who imaginatively affords, even as she delineates the risk to, and the loss of, "room for one's unknown" (Doll, 2017, p. 49); and Samuel Beckett, whose depiction of dialogical abundance, complexity, and failure[3] demonstrates that "talk defines the symbiotic condition of Being" (p. 54). I use the phrase "deeper conversation" advisedly, to express appreciation to Mary for encouraging me to engage the "depth work" of literary curriculum studies and to raise the question of the "dialogical depth" (Smythe, 2018) that characterizes Mary's writing and that of her readers.

Soon after my conversation with Mary, she gave me a most wonderful gift—her book *Beckett and Myth: An Archetypal Approach* (Doll, 1988). A work of literary criticism rather than curriculum theory, the book nonetheless addresses matters central to *currere*—in particular, the significance of venturing into psychic "material" that is "greater than the mere surface events of personal daily life," the alterity of which compels regression and the reawakening of the self (p. 12). *Beckett and Myth*, reflecting the literary and mythopoetic origins of Mary's curriculum theory, has inspired my thought about the intellectual movement that many scholars have made from literary studies to the curriculum field; and I have long thought of the book, Mary's gift, as an invitation to journey through the imaginary landscapes of literature into the study of *currere*.

After Mary gave me *Beckett and Myth*, however, for several years, I didn't read the book in its entirety. At first, I read only those passages in the book that addressed the works of Beckett that I knew well: *Waiting for Godot*, *Krapp's Last Tape*, and *Molloy*. I postponed a more thorough and linear reading, intending, I recall, to take it up as I became more familiar with Beckett's writing. My reading slowed. I waited. I ventured in the meantime of an incomplete reading. Slowness in reading, I would later learn, Mary greatly values, given that time, "a matter of attention, of attending . . . is where all the varieties of instants grow" (Doll, 2017, p. 50). Over time, in the interval before a complete reading, *Beckett and Myth* called to me, and I began to explore the book somewhat randomly, selecting pages and lines that caught my attention in particular moments and moods, and I lingered in the capacious subjective space the book afforded me, perhaps, like Gogo and Didi, as Mary describes their condition—in "unfamiliar territory," with "no guideposts," "waiting for instruction" (Doll, 2017, p. 53).

Reading Mary's text discontinuously, a remarkable dialogical complexity emerged, one enacted through my private study. I discovered the awing poetics of Mary's literary criticism, tracing its expression in her curriculum theory and the diverse intellectual milieu she engages. I followed her line of inquiry into Jungian thought, coming to understand ineffable experience as a necessary source of shadow and infinitude in everyday life. And I heeded the call of her literary commitment, the call to return to literature that challenges, animates, and "shows a way in the darkness"—"a way of sensing soul in the heart of things" (Doll, 1988, p. 73). As I entered the field of curriculum studies, *Beckett and Myth* laid bare literature as curriculum where I might encounter the otherness that constitutes the self, not as assimilable autobiographical meaning, but rather as enigmatic and necessary "objects, images, mirages, dreams, hallucinations, ghosts, [and] voices"—as "mantic speakings from the soul" that unsettle and renew the self (p. 14). Still, now, 20 years later, I pull *Beckett and Myth* from the shelf as though it were a collection of poems, taking it in hand for the distillations of being it contains, its potential for provoking thought, creativity, and becoming enhanced by an aleatory opening of its pages. "We do not experience being," Mary writes in *Beckett and Myth*,

> if we do not experience an objective reality that can rock us out of habit into the core of being's eddy. While the ego stonewalls us on earth, the psyche releases us into the rivers of all time. We should become more like the river and less like the rock if we are to discover being's source.
> (Doll, 1988, p. 14)

To read the writing of Mary Aswell Doll is to experience the fluidity of being as it emerges within the fissures of life's seemingly impenetrable structures. It is to know that "we are not removed from that which we study" (Doll, 2017, p. 142), the curriculum before us—Mary's writing—evoking complex "worlds-within" and the "imagination, wonder, [and] thought" to sustain them (p. 139).

We are not removed from that which we study, and yet a felt distance emerges. Perhaps it prevails. At times, certainly in my experience, it displaces entirely the pursuit of self-understanding and meaningful social worlds, the rock of the ego set mightily against the river of being. Mary's writing, however, is a counterforce to such alienation. It invites the fluidity of being necessary for authentic connection: intrapsychic, social, and ecological, as the writers in this volume demonstrate.

The metaphor of rock and water, so strikingly expressed in Mary's reading of Beckett, reappears in her 2000 book *Like Letters in Running Water*—a dedicated work of curriculum theory published shortly after my early conversation with Mary, and which soon became central to my teaching. In this brilliant text, imaginative landscapes again disclose the contours of the inner world, yet here literature is explicitly the site and source of educational experience, the lived curriculum understood as "an intense current within" (p. xii). Against the inner current stands the "blocked ego" (p. 81), securing its rocky terrain through literalism, that mode of interpretation that renders the "surfaces of our lives . . . so glassy bright that the undersurfaces are lost in the glare" (p. xiii). Where our meanings, our subjectivities, have become "like letters carved in rock" (pp. 1–80), Mary invites us to counter the "dangerous literalism" by reading imaginative literature, tapping into our "inner turmoil" (pp. xii-xiii), and venturing into "the running waters inside us, inside language, inside the cosmos" (p. 148). Becoming more like the river, oriented to being's source, we discover, is a life's work—the labor of *currere*.

We are a long way from Bill and Jeff's lovely holiday party, but still I feel the resonance of that early conversation with Mary, the generous and animated interpersonal dialogue threading through what I've come to know as the dialogical depth of her work. What is the dialogical character of Mary's scholarship and how does it inform this collection of essays?

I return to the rock and river. With this metaphor, writing from a Jungian perspective, Mary poetically depicts both the rigidity of the ego isolated from the fullness and abundance of the psyche—that is, its unconscious dimensions—and the need for encounters in the world, provocative and compelling in character, to lead us back to our inner depth. Reading imaginative literature, Mary argues, is an exemplary encounter for initiating such passage. I want to suggest that the expressive and aesthetic quality of Mary's own writing, so fully realized in *The Mythopoetics of Currere*,[4] also affords such movement—fostering rapport between the ego and otherness.

"One-sided though the ego inevitably is," the ego seeks and is called forth by its other, the Jungian analyst Mark Saban (2016) suggests. In a gloss of Jung's personification of unconscious contents, Saban explains that if the ego "possesses sufficient awareness and sufficient humility it can seek out a dialogical encounter with its own other, thus intentionally constellating inherent contradictions within the psyche" (p. 341). Situated precisely in this constellation of tensions, what Jung called the tension of opposites, Mary's work both expresses and evokes complex inner dialogue, illuminating the conditions of a "dialogical psyche," what Smythe (2018), in an elaboration of Jungian dialogism, describes as a psyche "constituted by a field of irreconcilable tensions among a plurality of polarities—conscious and unconscious, individual and collective, word and image, eros and logos, masculine and feminine, amongst a host of others" (pp. 452–453). The contributors to this volume, you will surely see, wholly engage the "plurality of polarities" within *The Mythopoetics of Currere* and extend the dialogical significance through their own engagements with theory, literature, and autobiography. In her book, Mary clarifies the conditions and stakes of such an endeavor: "Life is never without its opposite death, which is never without its opposite regeneration. No one thing, action, image, or idea is single; all is necessarily tensive and dynamic" (p. 136).

The dialogical depth of *The Mythopoetics of Currere* reflects Mary's thoroughgoing study of Jungian thought; it is not, however, reducible to Jung's own conceptualization of dialogue. On occasion, Jung depicted the psyche in specifically dialogical terms—the ego encountering the unconscious other "as if a dialogue were taking place between two human beings" (Jung, 1958, as cited in Smythe, 2018, p. 448). However, the notion of dialogue as a social, intersubjective, or even individually psychic event is not an "essential aspect of Jung's theoretical program" (Smythe, 2018, p. 449). In this vein, Smythe (2018) argues that Jung's dialogism is best grasped, not in his conceptual logic, but rather in his writerly expression, given that, in his writing—most dramatically in *The Red Book*—Jung "brought to bear the full range of symbolic forms characteristic of expression: poetic, literary, dramatic, pictorial, performative, and more" (p. 454). *The Mythopoetics of Currere* also exemplifies dialogism in its richness of expressive forms, "an unmistakable dialogical depth register" (p. 456) affording space for negotiating the psychical tensions it discloses.

Indeed, Mary begins the book with a poem of her own composition, "Mysterium Coniunctionis," a reference to Jung's idea that "events must possess an *a priori* aspect of unity" (Jung, 1963/1970, p. 464), as she evokes her own inner song, calling it "to sing the whirlwind" (p. ix).[5] From there, the song swirls, the expressive forms ramify. Mary delves into myth to bring forth memory; remembers her mother, father, and brother through encrypted histories, literary landscapes, and dreams; enters memory obliquely, free associatively, from multiple points of view; and roves through dreamscapes to generate thought about education's inner dimensions. Mary reads into being a web of discourses—curriculum theory, literary theory, cultural criticism, analytical psychology, myth, memoir, contemporary fiction, and more; and she threads it with her own autobiography—emergent, relational, daring, and open—establishing a place of study for her readers to grasp their own *currere* process. Mary shares substantial portions of her students' writings, enabling us to hear voices enlivened by depth work in humanities education and to grasp the significance of the deeply listening teacher. She interrogates cultural forms and modes of thought that bind subjectivity in conditions of hate and suffering, and she irradiates social and cultural complexity through the specificity of individual human expression. Mary critiques, jests, associates, narrates, digresses and returns via elsewhere, regresses to find queer passage into the social world, theorizes and ventures beyond the conceptual horizon, lyrically unwinds conceptual rigidity while establishing new landscapes of thought. Through it all, Mary expresses awe at the chaos, giving way to its force, shattering the stillness that arrests so the stillness of being, a continual becoming, might be found in the clearing.

The Mythopoetics of Currere proceeds through analysis of memories, dreams, and literary texts—this constellation of expressive forms called forth by Mary's deep and vibrant literary worldview. Understanding curriculum as a vast textual sphere, specified through subjective, social, and cosmological events and expressions of meaning, Mary calls us to read what is before us with ethical care and audacious spirit. The literary character of curriculum—the scene of education doubling as "the scene of reading" (Jacobus, 1999)—enables us to experience the self in education as it is animated and troubled by narrative and fictive forces, as it negotiates and gives way to otherness and the self's complex becoming. This is one of Mary's most important offerings to the field of curriculum studies. For Mary, imaginative literature situates the work of *currere*[6]—emplacing the lived curriculum and opening it inwardly. "Fiction connects readers with what courses within themselves," Mary explains (Doll, 2017, p. 48). "By discussing, selecting, and writing about ideas and images found in sufficiently difficult fictions," she continues, "student readers can recover their own curriculum" (p. 48).

Studying in the curriculum field, I have come to understand literature's unique curricular capacity,[7] a sense of educational experience still animated, via memory, by my early conversation with Mary so many years ago. If imaginative literature evokes inner experience recoverable as curriculum, it also unveils the interminability of that process of recovery, the aesthetic character of each literary text inviting a particular elaboration of one's subjectivity and each literary evocation of self-experience entailing the incompleteness of one's being. Writing *currere* through a literary landscape, we confront and must negotiate, even if unconsciously, the absence that constitutes our presence—something beckoning us, as Mary explains: "Something, a primal Unnamable self, a truth of another kind, [that] meanders within" (Doll, this volume). To heed the call of the unnamable self, I would suggest, is to awaken to, what Silverman (2000) terms, the "human imperative to engage in a ceaseless signification" (p. 146). *Currere* necessitates such awakening, as the writing of *currere* is an interminable project. What it also demands, then, is an enduring site and source for its inscription. Mary leads us, again and again, to its exemplary realm—the vibrant, complex, and enigmatic realm of literature.

Education thrives as it is lived in its depth and complexity, as it centers the subjectively experiencing person in the curriculum and animates the autobiographical dimensions of the process of study. Institutional education nonetheless diminishes subjective vibrancy and meaningful self-encounter where, through the standardization and decontextualization of knowledge, it severs "subjectivity . . . from the subjects taught" (Doll, 2017, p. 61), rendering the content of education lifeless in its availability to technical and instrumental manipulation. In response to such "educationism" (Doll, 2017, p. 61), curriculum scholars have conceptualized education as a process of self-formation and argued for modes of educational engagement and inquiry that animate and illuminate subjectivity in its embodied, individual, and relational specificity. Focused on this set of concerns, the contributors to this collection consider the unique and important way Mary advances thought about self-reflective subjectivity in education.

The first four chapters of the book explore several of Mary's key terms and metaphors, elaborating their significance within *The Mythopoetics of Currere* and in relationship to new sources and educational contexts. In Chapter 1, I address the "thread of meaning" that underlies Mary's curriculum theory text, demonstrating how the metaphor of the thread suggests connectedness along an obscure and meandering line of subjective associations as well as the form that emerges in the synthesis of disparate threads of experience. I also elaborate Mary's important contribution to curriculum studies in terms of her critical engagement with Jungian depth psychology, myth, her own autobiography, her students' writing and art, and a diversity of literary texts. Bill Pinar, in Chapter 2, reflects on the notion of "inscape" in Mary's writing, calling forth Mary's subjective presence as it is expressed through this and related concepts. Signifying subjective expression via "aesthetic, conceptual, and/or material form," the concept of inscape establishes a substantial "through-line" in Mary's work—from inner experience, which Mary explores in terms of dreams, emotion, and thought, to the outer world, which is vividly enacted in Mary's teaching. The significance of Mary's teaching, Bill elaborates, is demonstrated both as she magnifies the time, space, and fluidity of reading imaginative texts and as she invites students to "encode" their subjectivities in writing and art. In Chapter 3, Marilyn Hillarious engages environmental fiction, specifically Richard Powers' novel *The Overstory*, to demonstrate the expansive interpretive significance of Mary's theory of otherness in reading. Following Mary's notion of myths as "psychic stories," Marilyn explores the novel as myth, examining the psychical implications of modernity, technology, and globalization. Mary's mythopoetics of *currere* enables us to consider the poetics of the unconscious in tension with modernity's educational project; although the latter has diminished the imagination and care for a more-than-human world, Marilyn argues, Mary's project can help us reimagine environmental and intersubjective relationality and take up reparative "mythopoetic listening" to otherness circulating subjectively, socially, and ecologically. Molly Quinn, in Chapter 4, engages in a deep reflective reading of *The Mythopoetics of Currere*, accounting for the powerful subjective response that Mary's text evokes, situating the evocation of image, thought, and affect autobiographically and theoretically. Mary's thinking and writing tap into an inexpressible spirit, a "moreness," Molly argues, enabling us to linger at the limits of our thought and knowledge. Mary also "embodies, conjures, [and] incarnates" *currere*, performing its spirit and soul as a scholarly and autobiographical practice. Molly emphasizes the significance of reading in the mythopoetics of *currere* through her own autobiography—poetically rendered and situated in place—and through a synoptic close reading of the texts that animate Mary's thought. In Chapter 5, Mary Aswell Doll responds to her commentators, extending the dialogical event *The Mythopoetics of Currere* initiated. She attends carefully to the particular themes, images, and lines of inquiry that Bill, Marilyn, Molly, and I pursue in our chapters, while further contextualizing the "feminine consciousness" that subtends her work and that animates her intellectual, linguistic, narrative, and poetic expressions. Mary continues in an autobiographical voice, returning to the ruptures in being—the absences, losses, and opacities—that demand ongoing reflection in her *currere* process, further illuminating the "inscape" to be discovered in the writing of a life. Finally, Mary turns again to the myths, fictions, and fictive forces that center her study of *currere*, calling us once more to join her on a mythopoetic journey.

Notes

1. I have in mind Dwayne Huebner's (1993/1999) thoughts on "co-journeyers," which, like Mary's scholarship, animated my thinking when I was a doctoral student. "Life with others is never a substitute for the individuation required of us," Huebner writes. "Yet being with others on the journey is a source of hope, comfort, and love—all manifestations of the transcendent" (pp. 405–406).
2. See Sam Rocha's (2021) conceptualization of "the syllabus as curriculum" that both expresses "the *poesis* of teaching" (pp. 1–16) and evokes "the true teacher" who "speaks from within" (p. 211).
3. In *The Mythopoetics of Currere*, Mary provides a remarkable "catalogue [of] some of the kinds of talk in *Godot*" (Doll, 2017, p. 53). The list includes a wonderful range of communicative forms, including "logic, garble, and cataloguing" itself (p. 53). Mary shares the list, she explains, "not to exhaust the list (the list is endless) but rather to give an idea of the incredibly creative quality of these tramps to generate dialogue when there is really nothing else to keep them" (p. 53).
4. A compelling dialogism also permeates *Like Letters in Running Water* (Doll, 2000). In the book, Beckett reappears, his "explorations into the zero point" of language and meaning provoking awareness of the dialogical dynamics of the imagination, "where figures and events play out their drama" (Doll, 2000, pp. xiv, 85). From Beckett, Mary turns to other writers, like Jamaica Kincaid, whose "words [are] written to dislocate the mind" (p. 155), as she conceptualizes curriculum oriented to literature that values "sound rather than sense; that is, speakings that communicate through voice's timbre, language's rhythm, embodied gesture, and the melodies of conversation" (p. xix).
5. Copyright © 2017 From *The mythopoetics of currere: Memories, dreams, and literary texts as teaching avenues to self-study*. By Doll, M. A. Reproduced by permission of Taylor and Francis Group, LLC, a division of Informa plc.
6. "For me," Mary writes, "fiction in all its manifold manifestations is the place for the work that *currere* encourages" (Doll, 2017, p. 50).
7. See Chapter 15 of *The Mythopoetics of Currere*, "Capacity and Currere" (Doll, 2017, pp. 96–102).

References

Doll, M. A. (1988). *Beckett and myth: An archetypal approach*. Syracuse University Press.

Doll, M. A. (1997). Winging it. In T. R. Carson & D. Sumara (Eds.), *Action research as living practice* (pp. 1–10). Peter Lang.

Doll, M. A. (1999). Beyond the window: Dreams and learning. In W. F. Pinar (Ed.), *Contemporary curriculum discourses: Twenty years of JCT* (pp. 106–113). Peter Lang. (Original work published 1982)

Doll, M. A. (2000). *Like letters in running water: A mythopoetics of curriculum*. Lawrence Erlbaum Associates.

Doll, M. A. (2017). *The mythopoetics of currere. Memories, dreams, and literary texts as teaching avenues to self-study*. Routledge.

Huebner, D. E. (1999). Education and spirituality. In V. Hillis & W. Pinar (Eds.), *The lure of the transcendent: Collected essays by Dwayne E. Huebner* (pp. 401–416). Lawrence Erlbaum Associates. (Original work published 1993)

Jacobus, M. (1999). *Psychoanalysis and the scene of reading*. Oxford University Press.

Jung, C. G. (1958). The transcendent function. In S. H. Read, M. Fordham, & G. Adler (Eds.) & R. F. C. Hull (Trans.), *The collected works of C. G. Jung* (2nd ed., Vol. 8, pp. 67–91). Routledge & Kegan Paul.

Jung, C. G. (1970). The alchemical view of the union of opposites. In S. H. Read, M. Fordham, & G. Adler (Eds.) & R. F. C. Hull (Trans.), *The collected works of C. G. Jung* (2nd ed., Vol. 14, pp. 457–468). Routledge. (Original work published 1963)

Pinar, W. F. (1994). The method of *currere*. In W. F. Pinar (Ed.), *Autobiography, politics and sexuality: Essays in curriculum theory* (pp. 19–27). Peter Lang. (Original work published 1975)

Pinar, W. F. (2012). *What is curriculum theory* (2nd ed.). Routledge.

Rocha, S. D. (2021). *The syllabus as curriculum*. Routledge.

Saban, M. (2016). Jung, Winnicott and the divided psyche. *Journal of Analytical Psychology, 61*(3), 329–349. https://doi.org/10.1111/1468-5922.12225

Silverman, K. (2000). *World spectators*. Stanford University Press.

Smythe, W. E. (2018). Jungian dialogism and the problem of depth. *Journal of Analytical Psychology, 63*(4), 444–446. https://doi.org/10.1111/1468-5922.12428

1 Following the Thread of Life

Brian Casemore

Mary Aswell Doll (2017) proceeds in the labor of *currere* by following a thread. She follows the thread of life woven through memory and history, entangled in shadows and chthonic depths, unwound by literature, dream, and myth. In *The Mythopoetics of Currere*, the thread emerges as a theme and a fundamental element of her curriculum theory as she describes the influence of Carl Jung's autobiography on her own thought and "journey into the depths of . . . psychic being" (p. xi). In this context, she contemplates Jung's concept of synchronicity and the perception of reality it affords. According to Jung (1955/1991), synchronicities are acausal yet meaningful connections between psychic and material events, revealing the interrelationship between inner life and the external world. Doll explains that the experience of synchronicity provides passage into the dimensions of the self beyond ego, exposing the continuity in happenstance, the through line of life always partially obscured in the thicket of experience.

Synchronicities remind us, Doll (2017) explains, that "things happen and come together for a reason" outside the order of the ego (p. xii). In them, she finds the thread that connects: the thread coiled, meandering, and unfurled in the poetic reality of the unconscious[1] and yet made available to consciousness through dreams, associations, and imaginative thought.[2] Demonstrating this deeply subjective inquiry, Doll remembers the synchronicity of a dream she had in college, one that, she explains, foretold her father's death. It was "a dream," she writes, "that spoke so forcefully, with such clear and resounding images, that I knew it was truth of another kind" (p. xi).

Synchronicities shock us into awareness of the alterity of psychic life. Doll's work demonstrates that they can also initiate our journeying into the unconscious dimensions of experience. We see this as Doll pursues—through emotional complexity, courageous autobiography, and inspired study—the fuller fabric of meaning that her dream heralds. Although she mentions the dream only briefly in her initial reflections on Jung's autobiography, Doll (2017) returns to the dream in a chapter about her father and

DOI: 10.4324/9781003231547-2

her relationship with him, threading the line of unconscious significance through her conceptualization of forgetting, memory, and "regression," that is, "the first step backwards in *currere*" (p. 28). The synchronous dream invites this reflection and elaboration, we learn, because Doll's father "lived in [her] psyche," his death leaving her "adrift," the dream offering a promise of return (pp. 28–29). The dream, Doll explains, was "astonishingly true to the actual events that surrounded [her] father's last night," exposing the fragile yet vital thread that would lead her through the ghostly landscape of loss and to the recovery of his memory (pp. 28–29).

"One needs a thread," Doll (2017) explains, "to navigate the difficult passages of one's journey in life" (pp. xii–xiii). *The Mythopoetics of Currere* thus orients us to—indeed, immerses us in—intellectual and autobiographical journeying that follows the thread of life in the labyrinth of being: "the thread that connects one not only to the exit but to the entrance, to one's beginnings, even to the cord spun while in embryo, even to the archetypes found in myth" (p. xiii).

Doll's mythopoetic *currere* is a weave of vibrant strands, including Jungian depth psychology, curriculum theory, mythical story and image, personal autobiography, poetry, student writing and art, and literary culture and history. These strands are drawn together as Doll (2017) expresses her commitment to the inner world of the self as the fundamental source of curriculum understanding, "the pull of the inner life" (p. xi) so manifestly the animating force of her oeuvre.[3] *The Mythopoetics of Currere* illuminates key threads in Doll's larger body of work, revealing the uniqueness of her approach to *currere* study, while it also invites her readers more deeply into this realm of understanding curriculum, generating new language and metaphors for the "coursing" that is educational experience.[4]

Among the many metaphors enriching Doll's text, the metaphor of the thread most captivates my imagination in that it suggests connectedness along an obscure and meandering line of subjective associations as well as the form that emerges in the synthesis of disparate threads of experience: threadwork—web, weave, knot, and net—as the structure of being.[5] The numerous and subtly interwoven chapters of *The Mythopoetics of Currere* exemplify how following the thread of life through memory, dream, and literature—however protean and disquieting a journey—affords a complex and capacious structure for one's education, a sense of place for one's becoming. The duality of the thread—unwound and woven, both leading through the otherness of experience and coming to form as the locality of thought and subjectivity—registers the "two-ness" of Doll's (2017) *currere* (pp. 6–7, 83, 142). Emphasizing two-ness, Doll grounds her curriculum inquiry in Jungian thought, grasping the damaging nature—that is, the splitting force—of static dichotomies and therefore attending to the ineluctable tension between opposites and the imaginative potential of the dynamic in-between (Donati, 2019). The productive tension—between the conscious and the unconscious, the individual and the collective, ego and shadow, inside and outside, interiority and the public sphere—is found, in Doll's (2017) terms, where "two lines meet and in-fold" (p. 142). In this essay, I elaborate Doll's threadwork in terms of this two-ness and characterize dynamic tensions that express its significance.

The Thread of Life in the Labyrinth of Being

To follow the thread of life is to pursue a circuitous and uncertain course into lost or forgotten dimensions of the self, a course laid bare—only as it is lived[6]—in moments when "the waking mind lessens its focus" (Doll, 2017, p. 39) and the particulars of one's existence—"what one selects to write about, who one's friends are, what habits one has developed, the mistakes one makes, the people one hates" (p. xii)—become imbued with unconscious significance. Doll (2017) employs the mythological tale of Theseus and the Minotaur to demonstrate the symbolism of thread in the hero's journey, illuminating the threadlike character of the ego's connection with the unconscious: tenuous yet traceable, sinuous yet essential. In the myth, Ariadne gives Theseus a spool of thread to unravel during his passage into the labyrinth where the Minotaur, "hybrid of bull and human" (p. xiii), is caged; and Theseus, after killing the monster Minotaur, follows the thread where it lies unwound, retracing his path out of the darkness of the labyrinth.

As he insinuates himself into the labyrinth, Theseus unravels the thread, moving toward the monster—his family's monstrous, forgotten past[7]—where, in the otherness of the Minotaur's "hybrid face," he discerns "his own face reflected back to him" (Doll, 2017, p. xiii). For Doll (2017), this movement signifies the "regress" of *currere*: psychic movement "back into . . . buried material of shame, suffering, and memory" (p. xv). In Jungian terms, *currere* moves toward the shadow self that troubles the ego—the personal unconscious individually lived and expressed, and yet rooted in the collective unconscious. *Currere* unfolds, Doll suggests, as a "labyrinthine journey" toward "our personal monster" (p. xiii)—an aspect of the self-made monstrous "by the demands to bury what is not socially acceptable" (p. xv). The monster's lair, from the perspective of Greek mythology and Jungian thought, is a realm of chthonic forces: "human nature's instinctive drives and dark, rejected propensities," figured in myth as creatures and deities of the earth or underworld (Fontelieu, 2020, para. 3). Chthonic beings and their territories embody not only disavowed and fearsome memories and impulses but also arcane knowledge and creative energy that can renew the self. They unveil, paradoxically, "a fertile and divine source of abundance"

(Fontelieu, 2020, para. 3). "The underworld waits," Doll (2017) explains, "as our dreams and memories wait . . . to be stirred into awareness" (p. 7). *Currere*—in a mythopoetic register—leads us on an anfractuous passage into this chthonic domain; and however darkened the path or troubling the figure of our shadow self, the regression of *currere* provokes its own countermovement. When we are open to what the monster portends, encountering the dreadful monster of our psychic past "awakens"[8] the self, enabling us to discover the self's abundance, richness, and complexity.

The story of Theseus and the Minotaur, in its chthonic associations,[9] expresses the dual and mutually animating movements of Doll's *currere*. The monster Minotaur represents "the depths of the desires of the hidden self" in their terrifying excess—the monster "feeds on the children of Athens" (p. xiii), Doll (2017) explains—yet the Minotaur is also an "ocean of power and thrilling force that gives life meaning and makes art possible" (Powell, 2012, as cited in Doll, 2017, p. xiii).[10] This dynamic of opposing forces resonates deeply in Doll's writing. Like Theseus, she pursues the entwining thread of "mythic dichotomies" (p. xiii) so that she might "see anew what has been forgotten or repressed" (p. xv); doing so, she sets forth a theory and practice of *currere* profoundly attentive to the "two-ness in everything" (p. 142). "There is the past that is present, the other that is the self, the shock that becomes recognition," Doll explains: "Always two" (p. 142). The individuation of *currere* emerges then from mythopoetic care for this "two-ness"—openness to relational specificity enacted through one's singularity. As we meet the monster along the thread of our being, Doll teaches us, the monster "puts us in a different mind" (p. 100), inviting us to expand the fabric of our inner world and the places we inhabit. Engaged with chthonic forces, Doll's mythopoetic *currere* conjures dynamic, two-way movements: inner and outer, cohering and dispersing, regressing and emerging. In the remainder of this essay, I elaborate Doll's theoretical contribution to *currere* studies in these terms and offer close readings of chapters from *The Mythopoetics of Currere* that reflect the complex two-ness of her mode of inquiry.

The Two-Ness of Mythopoetic *Currere*

Doll engages and expands *currere* as a field of thought and practice of inquiry. She elaborates the concept as it was introduced by Bill Pinar and Madeleine Grumet (1976/2014) in *Toward a Poor Curriculum*, explores its use and evolution in subsequent curriculum scholarship (Grumet, 1978, 1999, 2016; Morris, 2001, 2015; Pinar, 1994, 2009, 2012; Salvio, 2007; Baszille, 2016), and specifies the mode of inquiry that illuminates *currere*: the curriculum as lived. As an approach to curriculum research, *currere* study engages lived experience and "the personal" through autobiography, understanding the elucidation of self-experience to be always partial, given an ineradicable subjective opacity. Doll (2017) uniquely and powerfully interprets this obscure dimension of *currere* through Jungian depth psychology as "the hidden other dimension that ghosts the self" (p. xii). Her introduction to the concept of *currere* through this Jungian framework indicates the distinctiveness of her project. "The urging of *currere* is to regress into . . . personal histories" obscured in the shadows, Doll explains, and this provocation of the cryptic past, discovered in and pursued through *currere* study, is reduplicated in the "call" of myth (p. xiii)—myth, that mode of writing that "open[s] our portals to what lies beyond, beside, or below the surface" (p. 66).

Though *currere* is fundamentally interior work, Doll makes clear that this mode of study is never solely so, as it requires, as well, a purposeful analysis of the self's entanglement with history, culture, the world. "*Currere* is Pinar's major (seminal) contribution to curriculum studies," Doll (2017) explains, "for its re-cognizing the self as an organizing entity that reaches out to reconceptualize the world" (p. 63). She elaborates, stating that as an "organizing entity," the self is structurally complex, divided against itself in its conscious and unconscious dimensions, ego and shadow. The organizing dynamism of the self thus provokes and blocks self-communication, requiring of the student of *currere* both a regressive turn to inner experience in its chaotic fluidity and a writerly emergence from that regressive "flow" (p. 62). In one of several remarkable close readings of Pinar's theory, Doll characterizes this act of writing as "a necessary second stage" of *currere* in which one conceptualizes the "remembered self with words" (p. 62), as her own writing in this regard, issuing from her own resurrection of ghosts, advances *currere* as imaginative, mythopoetic journeying between inner and outer worlds.

In Section One of the book, "Dreams and the Curriculum of the Remembered Self," Doll charts the movement of the mind in its perceptual contact with a "primitive self" (Pinar, 1994, as cited in Doll, 2017, p. 62) that cannot be wholly disclosed and yet that must be sought if personal meaning is to exceed the telling of selfsame stories. She explores memory and dreams to foster a necessary mode of "dwelling" in the "*un*familiar wellspring" of subjectivity (Doll, 2017, p. 4), entering the otherness of this psychic terrain with myth as her guide, given that "the psyche is mythic" and "myths are psychic stories" (p. xiii).

The chapter "Memory and *Currere*" is an exemplary demonstration of the mythopoetic foundations of Doll's curriculum theory and the two-ness of her practice of inquiry. The chapter explores the story of Odin from Norse mythology—specifically, Odin's journey to Mimir's well where he pledges an eye to drink from this well of wisdom and receive the mystic vision it imparts. Mimir is a giant whose severed head has been reanimated as the oracle of the well, his name denoting "memory"—in Old Norse, "the rememberer, the wise one" (Simek, 1993, p. 216). Mimir's well is located beneath and nourishes the Yggdrasil tree, the tree of life or "the great ash tree of the world" (Doll, 2017, p. 3). For a draught from the well, Odin makes the payment Mimir demands, sacrificing his own right eye. Odin's offering up the right eye is a mythopoetic detail that Doll (2017) contemplates in terms of "Left/Right symbolism," noting that the right eye, governed by the left brain, "controls logic, intellect, reason, and power" (p. 4). Surrendering the eye of rationality and literalism to the "Well of Memory," Odin seeks intuitive and imaginative capacities diminished, Doll carefully reveals, by the excesses of reason. Receiving Odin's eye in the watery realm of memory and wisdom, letting "the sacrificed eye sink deep into the water of the well," (p. 4), Mimir releases to Odin a wellspring of vision:

> Odin drinks from the well. As he drinks all the future becomes clear to him. He sees what will happen to the gods of Asgard and the humans of Midgard. He sees the great battle between good and evil that will play out at the doom of the gods. And he sees that evil will be destroyed so that a new era can emerge.
>
> (p. 4)

In the torment and transformation this myth conveys, Doll follows the thread of *currere*. In the surrender of the rationalizing eye to the depths of memory and the deliverance of the imaginative eye within the world, Doll detects the dual direction of *currere* as elaborated in Pinar's (2012) theory. Through the story of Odin, "clear in its sense of two-ness, right and left, conscious and unconscious," Doll (2017) explains, "we are being re-minded to observe our worlds with greater imagination but also to re-turn to the buried (repressed, forgotten) contents with greater insight, the 'mind' of the left eye" (pp. 6–7). Like Odin's search for wisdom, *currere* study requires and compels regression into memory, yet it reaches no end in the experience of inner dwelling. In its dual directedness, *currere* study engages the past as "the source-book for the future" (Pinar, 2012, as cited in Doll, 2017, p. 4), recovering memory, Doll explains, "to re-enter the public sphere" (p. 4).

Currere necessitates but finds no conclusion in remembrance via subjective regression. Nor does *currere*—the running, the coursing—culminate in a narrative representation of the self having so journeyed into the past. *Currere* proceeds in part through theoretical and scholarly distanciation, given that experience, taken as an exclusive authority, can "provincialize and even mislead" (Pinar, 2011, p. 17). But *currere* does not solve the messiness and uncertainty of experience by merely confirming theory—a theory of historical subjectification, for example—on the evidence of experience lived and recollected. Integrating dual purposes, subjective and social, autobiographical and allegorical (Doll, pp. 4, 7, 62), *currere* sustains a relationship with the enigmatic complexity of the self in the world, countering tendencies toward literalism in personal story and social-political theory (Pinar, 2011, pp. 17, 27, 34). In kind, Odin's myth, through the "murkiness" and "mystery" of its primary terrain of meaning, teaches that "hidden knowings are not meant to be grasped quickly by literal vision," given that the thread of life—the significance of our personal and collective histories—is to be found, Doll (2017) insists, in "that which cannot be clearly articulated" (p. 7).[11]

In the labor of self-study, Doll (2017) emphasizes, "it is not enough to move in one direction only," drawing attention to the way *currere* study elicits, intensifies, and pursues a fundamental dynamic of individual subjectivity: the recursive movement between self and world (p. 4). Through the figures of Odin and Mimir, Doll thus illuminates the specificity and significance of *currere* as a mode of inquiry dually engaged, not split but rather animated by study of private and public spheres of experience, subjective and social realms of engagement: animated, to use the Jungian phrase, by the "tension of opposites" (Jung, 1943/1953, p. 53). In the myth, such productive tension is depicted as Odin relinquishes his right eye to the underworld, releasing a chthonic wisdom, and as his left eye remains "above ground," providing the creative vision necessary to discern "the secrets of the runes" (p. 4). Here, Doll (2017) correlates the runes—symbols of arcane significance—with the objects and subjects of our study, that which we, students and scholars of curriculum, "must 'study' in the company of others to complicate our thinking about self and world" (p. 4).

Mythopoetic Study and Teaching

Mythopoetic study is exemplified by one of Doll's art students, Meredith, who, for the final project in a class on myth, created a painting in response to the Odin story. For the painting, Meredith used a canvas made from elephant dung, following, perhaps, the Nigerian British artist Chris Ofili in his use of the material as a "gut medium," situating creativity in the linked processes of devouring, absorbing, and rejecting (Awoyokun, 2013, p. 7). The choice of canvas evokes for me, as well, the labor of the dung beetle, or scarab, moving a ball of dung across the landscape, which appears in one of Carl Jung's visions (Burnett et al., 2013, p. 128).[12] In Egyptian myth, this work of the dung beetle symbolizes the movement of the sun across the sky and, thereby, rebirth and self-creation.[13]

On this canvas, Meredith painted the Yggdrasil tree, an interpretive, mythopoetic painting that unsettles and renews Doll's sense of the myth's significance. Engaged with Meredith's painting, enthralled by the creation,

Doll reconsiders the details of the myth (Hathaway, 2002, p. 57). Doll (2017) explains that Meredith

> painted every corner of the five-foot dung piece, highlighting the recognizable aspects of the tree, including the squirrel Ratatosk that runs up and down the trunk, connecting upper and lower realms; the Midgard serpent, encircling the Earth underwater; and the Fenrir wolf tied to a rock with a magic ribbon made of the roots of a mountain, the spittle of a bird, the breath of a fish, and the beard of the woman.
>
> (p. 5)

Doll lingers with these details of her student's work. The particulars are runic yet graspable, taken not as messages with "a one way trajectory" (Grumet, 2006, p. 48), nor as facts in a sphere of coherent meaning, but rather as expressions of educational experience, indeed curriculum, as Madeleine Grumet (2006) conceptualizes, both of the world and of the subjectivity it conveys.

As a teacher, Doll fosters the emergence of curriculum with lines of movement passing through inner and outer worlds, exemplifying, I believe, an image of curriculum that Grumet (1976/2014) introduces in *Toward a Poor Curriculum* and further elaborates in a more recent essay calling for education to provide passage to the world beyond schooling (Grumet, 2006). Grumet (2006) offers an image of perpetual movement between internal and external realities, reminding us that "at any given point we exist suspended between two worlds that we know only partially" (p. 48). She suggests, in Jungian terms, that curriculum as *currere* functions like a "lemniscate, or figure eight, ever enlarging human experience through its extension of both internal and external non ego" (p. 48). This image of continuous inner/outer movement, an infinite threading of alterities through experience, is vividly enacted in Doll's text. Throughout *The Mythopoetics of Currere*, Doll (2017) pursues with striking verve and vision, in her words, the "various states of otherness [that] lie ready to make claim and awaken consciousness to that which causes the ego to slumber" (p. 98). In her pedagogical engagement with Meredith's painting, she pursues the Yggdrasil tree to its metaphorical root, "the deeper stratum of the collective unconscious, the primeval psyche" (p. 7). Traversing the path of the lemniscate, Doll translates the "image awareness" that the painting affords into the world of the classroom, where, with her students, in the public sphere, she pursues "a common effort to restore Memory" (p. 7).

Reflective passage between inner and outer worlds, we learn from Doll (2017), demands inquiry that counters the force of "dangerous literalism," inquiry that dismantles the "modern myths without metaphors" that have "colonized our ways of thinking" (pp. 49–50). Doll thus calls us, and her students, to engage myths in their imaginative, fictive character, to engage "fiction in all its manifold manifestations" (p. 50), so that we might encounter their meanings as "a beckoning 'something'" (p. 126). Doll writes: "Myths and fairytales are so canny that their meanings are never overt but rather a beckoning 'something' we need to address" (p. 126).

Doll (2017) reveals her pursuit of the enigmatic "something" that beckons within her "inner currents" (p. 49). She does so through detailed accounts of her own reading process. Moreover, through careful accounts of her teaching, as we see in her engagement with Meredith, she reveals that "something"—the cryptic force or entity that ruptures literalism—to be the fundamental source of her pedagogy. As her student Meredith resymbolizes myth, Doll attends to the limits of symbolization, the animating otherness of *currere*, a curriculum—autobiographical in character and rooted in the humanities—as Grumet (2006) suggests, "teetering on the edge of what it means to be human" (p. 50). As a teacher of *currere*, taking up the expressive and interpretive work of her student, Doll epitomizes a humanities orientation to autobiography conceptualized by Grumet (2006): the teacher reading "to discern how another question or understanding would enlarge [an autobiography's] presentations of self and world" (p. 50). Attending to Meredith's painting of the Yggdrasil, Doll (2017) notes that the details of the painting "are so many and various that they attest to its psychodynamic" (p. 5). It is a curriculum that draws her to otherness without and within, a tree "though still, it moves; though solid, it is fluid; though grand, it is ominous," compelling her to declare in awe of its enigma and abundance: "This is not 'just' a tree" (p. 5).

Through her teaching, Doll creates a subjective clearing for the otherness her student conveys, the painted image of the tree giving way to its figurative and inexpressible plenitude. As Doll (2017) elaborates the educational event, she further demonstrates the seriousness and delight with which she regards Meredith's aesthetic study. She first notes that the painting evokes her memory of an element of the myth that does not in fact appear in the painting: the magical ribbon binding the Fenrir wolf. This image under erasure makes room for another important detail:

> Meredith was unable to paint the ribbon, I am relieved to say, since magic need not be re-presented. So complex and colorful was Meredith's painting, with rich browns, reds, and blues! But what spoke to me, caught my eye, turned my mind around, was . . . the eye of Odin. Meredith did not overlook the small detail of Odin's eye gleaming from the depths of the well of Mimir.
>
> (p. 5)

Doll follows the thread of *currere* through the dynamics of presence and absence, through the unrepresentable force of magic and the re-presented sacrifice of a part of the self. And Meredith, the student, returns to Doll, the teacher, "that strange other detail that lies in the dark waters of Memory" (p. 6). Doll writes:

> Up to that point in my teaching of the myth, I confess not to have paid attention to Odin's sacrificial eye. That Odin was recognized by an eye patch was enough detail for me. Teacher can explain and explain, but artist restores memory. I will not forget that moment in class. I was both delighted with Meredith's portrayal and dismayed by my own "intelligence," having forgotten this significant mythic motif of the eye in water.
>
> (p. 5)

Through the study of myth, and through our reception of our students' mythopoetic labor, Doll demonstrates, we can rediscover the dynamic tensions of *currere* that so complicate curriculum and our conversations about it: the regression into memory as a passage to futurity, the exploration of interiority as an outward opening to relationality and collectivity, and the engagement with our own subjectivity, in its indistinctness and mystery, as an encounter with otherness. In the study of myth, we see the elemental movement of *currere* toward otherness. "This is *currere*," Doll emphasizes, "a territory of the self both mine and not mine" (p. 4).

Familial Relationships and Mythic Kin

Myth enables exploration of this territory that exists both within and elsewhere. So too do memory and dreams afford passage into the alterity of *currere*. Throughout Section One of *The Mythopoetics of Currere*, Doll reveals the expanse of otherness, including its cultural and social dimensions, to be intimate in character, made available for study through memory of the relationships that shape us and interpretation of images that our dreams usher into consciousness. In auto/biographical narratives about her mother, brother, and father, Doll (2017) explores "memory tinged with the ghosts of unresolved tensions" (p. 27), the subtly imbued fabric of memory suggesting a pattern, a fundamental image of the self that, however unknowable, calls her "to plumb the depths of the undiscovered self" (p. 28).

Writing through personal memory, through the loss and longing of familial bonds, is a fundamental process of *currere*, one that acquires meaning, Doll (2017) argues, as it follows the thread of life toward "those figures from the deeper past who haunt us: the mythic ones" (p. 28).

Another quality of two-ness emerges, therefore, in Doll's *currere* study—the juxtaposition of familial relationships and mythic kin. Remembering her "larger-than-life mother," Doll (2017) turns to myth to expand the sense and sphere of connection with this woman, "Mother," an "exotic, smart, difficult woman" who, subject to the repressive gender norms of the 1940s, made "a claim for her life *as woman* [emphasis added]" (pp. 22–23). After her mother's death, Doll's writing through memory, she explains, intensified both her experience of "being a distant daughter to [her] mother" and her loss of the "mothering that other mothers could never give" (p. 22). While memory evokes the agony of separation, the Greek myth of Demeter and Persephone initiates passage into an enriching and complex mythopoetic curriculum, one that elucidates and complicates "the dynamic that exits between the hidden daughter and the powerful Earth mother" (p. 23). In its correlation with Doll's experience, however, the myth does not bring interpretive closure to her lived curriculum. There is no explanatory finality in Doll's grasping "Mother" as Demeter, herself as Persephone. Rather than comforting certitude, what myth—engaged through *currere*—affords her is a place of study: "a *subjective site* calling for . . . continual reengagement and reconstruction" (Casemore, 2017, p. 44).

Such a site emerges for Doll as she follows a thread of inquiry through subjectively significant ideas, images, and stories—all collocated in mythopoetic terrain. Remembering her mother, Doll (2017) associates from one mythic figure to another, turning from Demeter and Persephone—the latter's "descent into darkness" compelled rather than self-willed—to Inanna, the goddess of Sumerian mythology, "whose role as queen of heaven is humbled as she intentionally makes the journey into darkness to meet her other buried self" (p. 23). By her own choice, Inanna "must 'die' to her upper-worldly self-satisfaction in order to experience the agonies and nuances that 'live' in darkness" (p. 23). Although not a mother goddess,[14] Inanna is a female chthonic deity who intends her underworld descent, countering the subjugation of Persephone in Doll's autobiographical, mythopoetic curriculum,[15] and symbolizing a capacity for chthonic journeying that Doll shares with her mother. The goddess embodies an element of Doll's psyche that, when explored through the labor of *currere*, brings her closer to her mother, enabling her to articulate: "I am of her flesh and spirit" (p. 23).

Moreover, as Doll pursues the thread that connects familial and mythic kin, places are discovered, their "agonies and nuances" excavated, and new places—curricular places, places of study[16]—come into being. The spatial character of Doll's mythopoetic *currere*[17] is amplified in her account of studying the Inanna myth. It takes her, she emphasizes, "to where the chthonic female lives, in the moisturizing darknesses of the soul" (Doll, 2017, p. 23).

If following the thread of life exposes the tortuous path and chthonic complexity of a meaningful existence, it also transforms the practice of everyday life into world-making self-study. Of the Inanna story, Doll (2017) writes: "This myth tells me that my writings and myth teachings are pointing me, always deeper, into the undiscovered parts of myself in the mother-world" (p. 23). To follow the thread of life then too is to find passage from the shadows, with insight, into the world we inhabit with others.

Reading in a Mythopoetic Curriculum

In the second half of her book, "The Mythopoetics of *Currere* in Literary Texts," Doll (2017) brings heightened focus to teaching literature as a route into the self-study that is *currere*. The thread emerges here briefly as the spider's medium. Elaborating a line from Virginia Woolf's *A Room of One's Own*—"Fiction is like a spider's web, attached ever so lightly perhaps, but still attached to life at all four corners" (Woolf, 1929/1957, as cited in Doll, 2017, p. 47)—Doll emphasizes that the threadwork of literature reaches into the depths of experience. "The webbed connections fiction weaves go to the root of one's being," she writes, "if one will just let the spider spin" (pp. 47–48). In an earlier work, Doll (2000) gives sustained attention to the Native American legend of the Spider Woman (pp. 189–201) along with a nexus of archetypal women figures for whom web spinning is "a primal, even ludic occupation" (p. 193). There too, Doll's own "web spinning"— that is, threadwork—"begins in unknowing," proceeds through literary study, and, from the tension of opposites, establishes a sphere of complex meaning that serves as curriculum (p. 193). In the spirit of "recovering the feminine" (p. 194), Doll characterizes her labor of study and writing in a way that beautifully distills a core impulse of her larger mythopoetic *currere* project. "The thread I shall be weaving is not common," she writes: "It will join inners to outers, human to nonhuman, woman to bird to tree to worm to man to place" (p. 192). Section Two of *The Mythopoetics of Currere* manifests from this impulse, the practice of reading and the art of literature revealed as fundamental sources in the uncommon and ongoing synthesis that is *currere*.

Throughout the section, in conversation with other curriculum scholars who amplify the complexity of reading and literary study (Block, 1995; Greene, 1973, 1995; Grumet, 1999; Salvio, 2007; Sumara, 1996), Doll elaborates the probing of literature necessary to enliven its subjective and pedagogical potential. In her account, reading excavates "the fictions that layer the self" (Doll, 2017, p. 47). Conceptualizing such subjective reading, Doll (2017) counters the goal of so much schooled reading: "symbol hunting and theme grasping" toward the mastery of "some Thing" on a test, the hunting down and offering up of decontextualized literary "fact" (p. 48). Doll is nonetheless concerned with particulars; it is, for Doll, the subtle particulars of the lived experience of reading that initiate and sustain *currere* study. She calls us, therefore, to a reflective, autobiographical mode of reading in which "one might remember one's pause, one's momentary, tiny questioning of firm, presentable understanding, one's ever-so-small crack into chiseled belief systems" (p. 49).

Reading as a practice of *currere* finds in images and metaphors—"the basic givens of psychic life" (Doll, 2017, p. xvi)—a structure of meaning in which enigma upends the known, in which the familiar gives way to the strange. Through such reading, "feelings thought to be central get routed," "peripheral imaginings begin to take root," and "one learns about living, about mistakes, and about being coerced by cultural demands" (Doll, 2017, p. 48). Journeying in the figural complexity of literature also "requires readers to tap into their inner turmoil, their coursings," and to witness internally forces of social demand and social antagonism (Doll, 2017, p. 48). It is, a practice of inquiry, therefore, that sustains our efforts "to grasp more coherently the world within as well as without" (Doll, 2017, p. 48). When deeply engaging the figurative threads of literary texts and their shadowed histories, reading becomes, Doll (2017) demonstrates, a venture into the symbolic terrain that interweaves fiction and reality, enabling one to "dwell a while in the dark" (p. xv) and to "unearth one's own foundational images" (p. xvi). Unearthing the images that organize the psyche makes them available for resymbolization and further study—in both private and public spheres of educational experience.

Doll (2017) thus deepens our grasp of not only the subjective foundations but also the social and political dimensions of literary study, further elaborating the transformative character of literary experience. "Out of the very chimney corner from which the humanities huddle," she reminds us, "fiction disturbs the status quo" (p. 47). Throughout the chapters of "The Mythopoetics of *Currere* in Literary Texts," we encounter literature that provokes unruly interpretive practices, as Doll demonstrates a mode of literary engagement that sustains their disruptive potential. Her commitment to this intellectual, autobiographical, and pedagogical labor is evidenced strikingly in the chapter "I am Dirt: Disturbing the Genesis of Western Hegemony." In this essay, a rupture of order in a culturally dominant narrative invites Doll to complicate the study of human origin and to specify subjectivity as the site and source of an education that expands and potentially transforms the world.

In "I am Dirt," Doll (2017) explores the shadow text of the "religious doctrine" of the West: "a dark underbelly known as myth, hidden or stamped out from modern Western consciousness" (p. 58). The reading

Doll undertakes in this chapter unravels the knots of a culturally hegemonic narrative and taps the fictive force of the mythical understanding that the dominant narrative conceals. More specifically, Doll interrogates the cosmogony of The Book of Genesis, engaging this "founding story of Western Eurocentric cultural values," first, toward discerning its legacy: "sowing the seeds of misogyny which forever splits off humans from earth, man from woman, and humans from animals" (p. 58). She then pursues this compelling deconstructive critique toward recovering the modes of relating, communicating, and being-in-time occluded by the ideology embedded in Genesis: the Great Chain of Being (pp. 56–57).

Citing Genesis, specifically God's call to the newly created man to "have dominion" over all creatures and things, "over all the earth" (*King James Bible*, 1769/n.d., as cited in Doll, 2017, p. 56), Doll traces the links between this theology of dominance and the acts of naming, categorizing, and dividing that are normalized and valorized in Western thought. In Genesis, Doll (2017) explains, "Logos, not Eros, rules, meaning that things must be separated and divided logically" (p. 56). This dominant narrative of human origin thus splits hierarchically light and dark, man and nature, man and woman (p. 56). The gendered implications run deep, Doll continues, as "woman, sculpted from the unconscious Adam's rib, is clearly a second thought, a possession really, and [she is] given no naming powers such as those given to Adam" (p. 57).

In this context, Doll reveals and enacts the power of undoing a narrative, a knowing, a name. She first briefly references the "postmodern, feminist Eve" of Ursula K. Le Guin's (1996) short story "She Unnames Them"—Eve, in this version, "unnaming the animals so as to free them" (Doll, 2017, p. 57). Doll then proceeds in a similar labor of deconstruction: reading other, early cultural myths of origin, using them to unbind the fundamental terms of Western cosmogony.

Doll (2017) recalls that the Adam of Genesis "quickly rises out of the dirt to subdue, rule, and name," compelling her to chart this "dirt origin" to "early mythic and spiritual cosmogonies" (p. 57). She takes up the story of the child Krishna, of Hinduism, holding all of existence in dirt in his mouth; the story of Spider Woman, from Southwestern Native American cultures, "mixing four piles of earth—white, black, yellow, and red—with saliva and mold[ing] these piles into the shapes of humans, singing them into creation"; and the story of Obatala, from the Yoruba religion, who descends from the sky, piling earth into chaos, and creating humans from the earth scratched up by a rooster (p. 57). In Doll's reading, as the dirt spreads around the tale of Eden, the lessons of Genesis—"dominion, obedience, punishment, and debasement (p. 57)—give way to the "tension of opposites" (p. 59), the serpent, once split off as evil, "reclaiming its connection with Earth and woman and reminding woman to do the same with the snake" (p. 57). Ultimately, in the goddess cultures, Doll finds the significance of "the snake-woman connection":

> In myth, opposite worlds blend together, need each other, act in tensive union; the cycle of life necessarily includes the underworld, and woman is not just a rib but a force of creation. A chthonic animal of the earth's darkness, the snake was once thus highly honored by goddess cultures and endowed with the wisdom of hidden knowledges. As an ancient symbol of rebirth, the snake literally sheds its skin to appear young, born again, when it emerges out of its year hibernation in Earth.
>
> (p. 58)

The rejuvenation of the snake figures powerfully the dual movement of Doll's mythopoetic *currere*, drawing from the chthonic domain a darkness that illuminates, an underworld force that renews being-in-the-world. It emphasizes, as well, the gendered character of such earthy curriculum and its obscure sources of knowledge. "Woman's connection to earth is thus older than Genesis," Doll elaborates, "and true knowledge is really wisdom which comes from unseen places" (p. 58).

The story of Genesis "put[s] an evil cast on both [snake and women], punishing all of humankind for women's curiosity" (p. 58), but Doll (2017) reads it askance, following the tendrils of this narrative thicket to its rootstalk, finding in preclassical myths, including the Pelasgian myth of Eurynome, that the snake is "webbed to the finer points of the cosmos" (p. 57) and that woman, figured as a snake, is the agent of creation, connection, and change. In this reading, Doll does not seek and express a superordinate counternarrative, acknowledging that all cultural myths do not undo the violence of the gendered splitting of Genesis. She pursues instead the countervailing forces of multiplicity, complexity, and flux. More specifically, she explores language and story from various tribal cultures that undermine the hegemony of Western "hierarchy, mastery, and logic" (p. 59) through productive tensions rather than splitting. Doll also counters the risks of essentialism in references to "indigenous knowledge" and "Western Eurocentrisms" (p. 60). She does so by enumerating a host of contemporary writers and scholars whose literature and theory enable us to find difference, complexity, and tension within culturally delimited fields of knowledge and aesthetic production: "Jamaica Kincaid, Hua Zhang, Lisa See, Shirley Geok-lin Lim, Maxine Hong Kingston, homi bhabha, Kwame Appiah, Jacque Daignault, [and] Hongyu Wang" (p. 60). The voices of these writers, and the productive tensions they sustain, imbue Doll's book as she threads them through her own *currere* study.

Conclusion: Otherness Within and Elsewhere

The journey within leads to the world without—the thread of life unwound in the labyrinth of being retraced to an outside expanded and complicated, unsettled and renewed. If the spatial metaphor of our psychic journey animates the unconscious significance of our material surroundings, it also reminds us that the physical and social spaces we inhabit—geography, architecture, and cultural landscape—demand our study of their histories, political effects, and subjective implications. "Place is the formation of character" (p. 142), Doll (2017) emphasizes. Analysis of the world that emplaces us, therefore, is an essential practice of *currere*.

Curriculum generated through such analysis "not only represents a 'place,'" Pinar (1991) explains, "it also becomes a 'place,' a curricular embodiment and contradiction" of socially and subjectively situated experience" (p. 165). Pinar's concern with "contradiction" in his early study of the curriculum of place foreshadows his later theorization of "the subject's noncoincidence with itself," subjectivity "imprinted [but not totalized] by culture, nationality, and by historicality itself" (Pinar, 2011, p. 11). Self-difference precedes how we proceed in the world. An internal alterity established, evoked, and provoked by an otherness beyond ourselves—by and from an elsewhere—"requires us," Pinar (2011) argues, "to enact the non-coincidence of subjectivity with reality through the cultivation of distance, even estrangement and exile" (p. 17). In *The Mythopoetics of Currere*, Doll (2017) brilliantly elaborates this project, poetically rendering the call from beyond as the reanimating force of the place within. "Traveling within takes us to uncharted territory," she writes: "Let us keep the vagueness of this place alive. The something of somewhere must beckon somehow" (p. 128).

Toward concluding my study of Doll's work, I'd like to reflect briefly on her reading of Shirley Geok-lin Lim's (1996, 1998) memoir and poetry—a literary engagement that magnifies the otherness of mythopoetic *currere* in terms of place, as "Elsewhere" (Doll, 2017, pp. 103–109). Writing about Lim, Doll (2017) explores the "several alienations that define her poetics of elsewhere: West and East, Mother and Father, men and women, violence and shame" (p. 101). Lim grew up in the British colony of Malacca, Malaysia—the child of a Chinese father and Peranakan mother—and she ultimately moved to the United States. In her poetry and memoir, Lim captures her "sense of being an outsider-within" (p. 103), negotiating life within her multiracial colonized homeland and then within the alienating forces of "the land of opportunity" (p. 107). Living always "elsewhere," Lim translates the toxic nourishment of her Western education into a path of individuation, writing in her memoir:

> I have seen myself not so much sucking at the teat of British colonial culture as actively appropriating those aspects of it that I need to escape

that other familial/gender/native culture that violently hammered out only one shape for self. I actively sought corruption to break out of the pomegranate shell of being Chinese and girl.

(Lim, 1996, as cited in Doll, 2017, pp. 104–105).

Doll elaborates this remarkable account, specifying the tension that rouses such complex becoming: "[Lim] is both East and West, neither all one or all other, neither one in clear dialogue with the other" (p. 104). Living such an in-between unmoors us from place. However, as Lim's autobiographical writing demonstrates, and Pinar (2011) suggests, the process of study that engages the otherness within and elsewhere "becomes a 'place'" (p. 165), an inhabitable sphere of meaning, a curriculum, that fosters an ongoing process of subjective deconstruction and emplacement. "It would seem, then," in Doll's (2017) terms, "that Shirley Geok-lin Lim has turned the Elsewheres of place, family, and gender into a new poetic sense of homeland" (p. 108).

For Doll, the tension of opposites, drawn forth from literary sources like Lim's poetry and memoir, animates *currere* in its fundamental movement. Splitting, like that enacted in The Book of Genesis, suppresses its force and potential. Genesis demands "separation from rather than co-operating with cosmos and world," Doll (2017) explains, and there is a correlate in "educationism" that severs "subjectivity . . . from the subjects taught" (p. 61). Doll thus warns against education that wholly abstracts knowledge, undermining the depth, specificity, and complexity of individual subjectivity.

What *currere* offers in this context is the recovery of the self that "the abstract individual has suppressed but not escaped"—recovery of the "primitive self" that stirs in the shadows of experience (Pinar, 1994, as cited in Doll, p. 62). Through the labor of *currere*, Doll (2017) argues, "the self, recovered by various means . . . is birthed from the dark, and like the myths of old, brings special wisdom, which must be translated and analyzed" (p. 63). As Doll demonstrates throughout her text, the student of *currere* pursues such insight and inquiry toward self-transformation *and* political engagement, enabling subtle and powerful movement between the primitive self and the public sphere. To emphasize this movement and relationship, Doll returns to Pinar's notion of "allegory" (p. 62). She explains that the term designates the relationship between the realm of the personal, which is always charged with unconscious meaning, and the realm of the conceptual, which is always exceeded by the worldly forms that our concepts name. Pinar nonetheless situates allegory in the sphere of subjectivity, thus sustaining the tension of social, historical, and cultural otherness in the sphere of the "living 'I'" (p. 62). Allegory therefore magnifies the relational character of *currere*, reminding us that this subjective labor of study illuminates "the connection humans have always had with other worldly forms" (p. 62). Through the notion of allegory, Doll explains, "Bill Pinar reconceptualizes for postmoderns what premoderns have always known: humans are co-operators with their worlds" (p. 62).

Here, in the relational vibrancy of *currere*, Doll invites us into mythopoetic inquiry that reveals the "capacity," indeed the "interiority," "within all things" (p. 96). Attending to the worldly forms of literature and myth, she orients us to "the reality that lies *underneath* words" (p. 139), broadening our sense of the world's "inner" complexity, expanding our grasp of the sphere of unfolding selfhood. In *The Mythopoetics of Currere*, moreover, Doll demonstrates how memory, dreams, and literary texts productively unsettle regimes of knowledge rigidified through literalism. Narrow orders of truth and being, we learn, give way to the capaciousness of subjectivity—that is, when subjectivity is opened to the forces of regression, reverie, and reading. Doll calls us to witness the diminished interiority of a world forged not only through literalism but also through rage, egoism, and authoritarian compliance, calling us, as well, to explore the capacity of mythopoetics to open inward through the "rupture of structures" held in place by assumed knowledge and values (p. 101). "Interiority" is, Doll explains, "that which is within all things and so has 'capacity'" (p. 96). The mythopoetics of *currere* then has a unique reflexive capacity: to recover interiority, to enliven the coursing within, and to help us find the thread of life in "the other inner side of things" (p. 96).

Notes

Author's note: An earlier version of this chapter was first published as Casemore, B. (2019) "Following the Thread of Life in Mary Aswell Doll's The Mythopoetics of Currere," *Journal of the American Association for the Advancement of Curriculum Studies*, 13(2). The author is grateful to the co-editors at JAAACS, Susan Mayer and Patrick Roberts, for their invitation to review Mary Aswell Doll's book for the journal.

1. In Chapter 8, "Beyond the Window: The Inscape of *Currere*," Doll (2017) explicates the poetic reality of the unconscious in these terms: "The unconscious is a poetic not a scientific reality. It can only be apprehended in an 'as if' manner, through personification and metaphor. So embedded are we in orthodoxy, however, that most of us are ignorant of the poetic nature of inner life—just as we are unaware of the rich deviations of our own cultures that draw on fantasy and imagination. The task of the teacher, as for the analyst, is to teach how to read psychic speech if the individual is to be brought together with the nurturing symbols of culture" (pp. 38–39).
2. The concept of synchronicity is not otherwise elaborated in *The Mythopoetics of Currere*. Doll's writing nonetheless conveys the way she works with synchronicities as pathways to insight, imagination, and the poetic reality of the unconscious.
3. One can chart Doll's sustained attention to questions of interiority from her early scholarship in literary criticism to her current writing in curriculum studies. In *Beckett and Myth: An Archetypal Approach*, Doll (1988) explores the "soul searching" in Samuel Beckett's body of work. Reading Beckett through myth and Jungian depth psychology, Doll provides a truly stunning account of his call

to inner experience: "Beckett takes us to various places, where soul—glimpsed but not found—is felt at its zero point. Empty rooms and ancient ruins become places that induce a thinking mind to cease for a moment its tiresome habit of figuring things out, always to conclusion, and to feel, for a change. There, in the space that emptiness affords, the living soul suffers. There, the searched-for soul lives" (p. 2). In *Like Letters in Running Water—a substantial contribution to curriculum studies, literary criticism, and humanities education*—Doll (2000) tells us curriculum is "a coursing, as in an electric current," a prelude to her account of the labor of curriculum theory: "The work of the curriculum theorist should tap this intense current within, that which courses through the inner person, that which electrifies or gives life to a person's energy source" (p. ix).

4. In *The Mythopoetics of Currere*, Doll employs and extends the metaphor of curriculum as an electric current, a coursing—a metaphor she first elaborated in *Like Letters in Running Water* (Doll, 2000). More specifically, in Chapter 7 of *The Mythopoetics of Currere*, Doll pursues the interior condition of curriculum by tapping the current of her dreamlife, recalling and interpreting dreams to "make the descent into dream power" (p. 34). Dreamwork, here, emerges as a fundamental practice of *currere*, as a fundamental approach to studying "the coursings from within" (pp. 34–37).

5. In this regard, Doll's textual threadwork resembles the textile-themed art of Louise Bourgeois, whose exploration of inner experience via painting, drawing, and sculpture reveals the threadlike line of creation to be "not just a trace or a thread," but "also a foundation, the basis for some sort of construction . . . a house, a web, a book, or an archive" (Oliveira, 2017, p. 24).

6. On curriculum as lived experience, see Aoki (1986/2005, 1993/2005) and Pinar (1994, 2011). Characterizing the integration of lived experience and intellectual labor, Doll describes the writing that disengages from regression, the backward movement of *currere*, while sustaining its significance. Referencing an earlier book (Doll, 2000), Doll (2017) explains: "This is like letters written in running water . . . where analysis emerges from a primal origin to convey the confluence of lived experience with consciousness and study" (p. 62).

7. Following Powell (2012), Doll (2017) writes: "Recall that Ariadne's father, Minos, was the son of Europa and a bull; that Minos was the uncle of Theseus; that some say Theseus was the son of Poseidon; that Uncle Minos 'forgot' to give sacrifice to Poseidon when a white bull was offered to him as a gift; that Poseidon, angered by Minos' forgetfulness, infused the wife of Minos, Pasiphae, with a lust for the white bull so intense that she demanded to consummate her desire, thanks to Daedalus, who crafted a fake cow for her to climb into. The result of the bull's impregnation of Pasiphae hiding her back side inside the crafted cow is none other than the birth of the Minotaur, half bull/half human" (p. xiii).

8. Doll writes: "I believe the monster's function awakens one to what lies below, slumbering" (p. 100).

9. "In Greek mythology," Dietrich (1973) explains, "the bull was considered a chthonic animal, and as such was closely related with cave cult" (p. 115). Some sources characterize Poseidon, father of the Minotaur, in chthonic terms (e.g., Dietrich, 1973, p. 185). In the context of analytical psychology, Savitz (1991) explains, "Poseidon, who sends the dazzling white bull, is the divine force and overarching symbol behind the Cretan labyrinth myth; he fuels the desire for power, love, beauty, heroic victory, and divinity, and shatters the world for all those who pursue it" (p. 466).

10. Moreover, the larger myth of the labyrinth, Savitz (1991) explains, "is filled with ambiguity and doubleness: it pairs love and abandonment (Theseus and Ariadne) and love and death (Daedalus and Icarus) so that moments of fulfillment are suddenly reversed and end in loss, emptiness, and despair. A chiaroscuro effect is created in which love and loss, the divine and human, the beautiful white bull and the monstrous, devouring minotaur are set off and seen in relationship to each other" (p. 466).

11. In *The Character of Curriculum Studies*, Pinar (2011) elaborates the conditions of our always partial grasp of experience: "It is the structural noncoincidence of the alive body—the time and space of subjectivity—that invites us to experience *experience*, for example, to remember what we have undergone, to forget what we cannot bear to remember, and to understand what we can recall and feel compelled to comprehend" (p. 8).

12. A scarab appears, as well, in Jung's (1955/1991, p. 31) well-known example of synchronicity—his patient recounting a dream of a golden scarab and then a scarab tapping at the window behind him and ultimately flying into the room.

13. In her discussion of dreaming in Chapter 7, "Dreams: The Coursings from Within," Doll describes the Egyptian god Ra moving the sun across the sky, labor requiring that at sunset, he "descend into a dark place where he [has] to confront the monster Apep" (p. 34). The journey into darkness that enables the return of the sun and the light—Doll likens this journey to dreaming. Facing the monster in the dark, the god Ra requires protection from the lion goddess Bast; in the journey into darkness that is dreaming, Doll tells us, each night, she "hop[es] the lion will lead the way" (p. 34).

14. Black and Green (1998) write: "The goddess Inana or Ištar was the most important female deity of ancient Mesopotamia at all periods. . . . Inana is not a goddess of marriage, nor is she a mother goddess. . . . In art, Inana is usually represented as a warrior-goddess, often winged, armed to the hilt, or else surrounded by a nimbus of stars" (pp. 108–109).

15. "Persephone is eternally the princess bride to the king of Hades," Doll (2017) explains, "the innocent one raped: her descent into darkness was not one that she willed" (p. 23).

16. In "Curriculum as the Place of Study" (Casemore, 2017), I elaborate Pinar's theory of the significance of place in curriculum. See also Grimmett's (2017) essay "Two Groundbreaking Ideas of William F. Pinar: Curriculum as Complicated Conversation and Study as the Site of Education."

17. Relevant to the spatial character of mythopoetic *currere* study, Doll (2017) comments on Jung's intense journey into unconscious experience: "call this place the unconscious, the otherworld, or the world of spirits. Below—earth journey stories of myth, dream, and vision offers writers and speakers the opportunity to tap other dimensions of time and space" (p. 61).

References

Aoki, T. T. (2005). Legitimating lived curriculum: Towards a curricular landscape of multiplicity In W. F. Pinar & R. L. Irwin (Eds.), *Curriculum in a new key: The collected works of Ted T. Aoki* (pp. 199–215). Lawrence Erlbaum. (Original work published 1993)

Aoki, T. T. (2005). Teaching as in-dwelling between two curriculum worlds. In W. F. Pinar & R. L. Irwin (Eds.), *Curriculum in a new key: The collected works of Ted T. Aoki* (pp. 159–165). Lawrence Erlbaum. (Original work published 1986)

Awoyokun, D. (2013). Neomodernism: Chris Ofili and the art of fugue. *Critical Interventions: Journal of African Art History and Visual Culture, 7*(1), 5–28. https://doi.org/10.1080/19301944.2013.10781424

Baszille, D. T. (2016). Haunting revelations. In M. A. Doll (Ed.), *The reconceptualization of curriculum studies: A festschrift in honor of William F. Pinar* (pp. 8–16). Routledge.

Black, J., & Green, A. (1998). *Gods, demons and symbols of ancient Mesopotamia: An illustrated dictionary*. The British Museum Press.

Block, A. (1995). *Occupied reading: Critical foundations for an ecological theory*. Garland.

Burnett, L., Bahun, S., & Main, R. (Eds.). (2013). *Myth, literature, and the unconscious*. Karnac Press.

Casemore, B. (2017). Curriculum as the place of study. In M. A. Doll (Ed.), *The reconceptualization of curriculum studies: A festschrift in honor of William F. Pinar* (pp. 42–49). Routledge.

Dietrich, B. C. (1973). *The origins of Greek religion*. Walter De Gruyter.

Doll, M. A. (1988). *Beckett and myth: An archetypal approach*. Syracuse University Press.

Doll, M. A. (2000). *Like letters in running water: A mythopoetics of curriculum*. Lawrence Erlbaum Associates.

Doll, M. A. (2017). *The mythopoetics of currere: Memories, dreams, and literary texts as teaching avenues to self-study*. Routledge.

Donati, M. (2019). From active imagination to active life: At the roots of Jungian social activism. *Journal of Analytical Psychology, 64*(2), 225–243.

Fontelieu, S. (2020). Chthonic deities. In D. A. Leeming (Ed.), *Encyclopedia of psychology and religion*. Springer. https://doi-org.proxygw.wrlc.org/10.1007/978-3-030-24348-7_113

Greene, M. (1973). *Teacher as stranger: Educational philosophy for the modern age*. Wadsworth.

Greene, M. (1995). *Releasing the imagination: Essays on education, the arts, and social change*. Jossey-Bass Publishers.

Grimmett, P. P. (2017). Two groundbreaking ideas of William F. Pinar: Curriculum as complicated conversation and study as the site of education. In M. A. Doll (Ed.), *The reconceptualization of curriculum studies: A Festschrift in honor of Professor William F. Pinar* (pp. 67–75). Routledge.

Grumet, M. (1978). Songs and situations. In G. Willis (Ed.), *Qualitative evaluation* (pp. 274–315). McCutchan.

Grumet, M. (1999). Word worlds: The literary reference for curriculum criticism. In W. F. Pinar (Ed.), *Contemporary curriculum discourses: Twenty years of JCT* (pp. 233–245). Peter Lang.

Grumet, M. (2006). Where does the world go when schooling is about schooling? *Journal of Curriculum Theorizing, 22*(3), 47–54.

Grumet, M. (2014). Existential and phenomenological foundations. In W. F. Pinar & M. Grumet (Eds.), *Toward a poor curriculum* (3rd ed., pp. 31–50). Educator's International Press. (Original work published 1976)

Grumet, M. (2016). The politics of presence. In M. A. Doll (Ed.), *The reconceptualization of curriculum studies: A festschrift in honor of William F. Pinar* (pp. 76–83). Routledge.

Hathaway, N. (2002). *The friendly guide to mythology: A mortal's companion to the fantastical realm of gods, goddesses, monsters, and heroes*. Penguin Books.

Jung, C. G. (1953). On the psychology of the unconscious. In C. G. Jung (Ed.) & R. F. C. Hull (Trans.), *The collected works of C. G. Jung* (Vol. 7, pp. 1–119). Princeton University Press. (Original work published 1943)

Jung, C. G. (1991). *Synchronicity: An acausal connecting principle*. Routledge. (Original work published 1955)

King James Bible. (n.d.). *King James Bible Online*. www.kingjamesbibleonline.org/ (Original work published 1769)

Le Guin, U. K. (1996). She unnames them. In S. M. Gilbert & S. Gubar (Eds.), *The Norton anthology of literature by women: The traditions in English* (3rd ed., pp. 1943–1945). W. W. Norton & Company.

Lim, S. G. L. (1996). *Among the white moon faces: An Asian-American memoir of homelands*. The Feminist Press at the City University of New York.

Lim, S. G. L. (1998). *What the fortune teller didn't say*. West End Press/University of New Mexico Press.

Morris, M. (2001). *Curriculum and the Holocaust: Competing sites of memory and representation*. Routledge.

Morris, M. (2015). Currere as subject matter. In M. F. He, B. Schultz, & W. H. Schubert (Eds.), *The SAGE guide to curriculum in education* (pp. 104–109). SAGE.

Oliveira, M. (2017). Weaving the archive: Some notes on the artist's books of Louise Bourgeois. *Journal of Artist Books, 42*, 24–28.

Pinar, W. F. (1991). Curriculum as social psychoanalysis: On the significance of place. In J. L. Kincheloe & W. F. Pinar (Eds.), *Curriculum as social psychoanalysis: The significance of place* (pp. 165–186). State University of New York Press.

Pinar, W. F. (1994). *Autobiography, politics, and sexuality: Essays in curriculum theory 1972–1992*. Peter Lang.

Pinar, W. F. (2009). *The worldliness of a cosmopolitan education: Passionate lives in public service*. Routledge.

Pinar, W. F. (2011). *The character of curriculum studies: Bildung, currere, and the recurring question of the subject*. Palgrave Macmillan.

Pinar, W. F. (2012). *What is curriculum theory* (2nd ed.). Routledge.

Pinar, W. F., & Grumet, M. (2014). *Toward a poor curriculum* (3rd ed.). Educator's International Press. (Original work published 1976)

Powell, B. B. (2012). *Classical myth* (7th ed.). Pearson.

Salvio, P. M. (2007). *Anne Sexton: Teacher of weird abundance*. SUNY Press.

Savitz, C. (1991). Immersions in ambiguity: The labyrinth and the analytic process. *Journal of Analytical Psychology, 36*(4), 461–481.

Simek, R. (1993). *Dictionary of Northern mythology* (A. Hall, Trans.). DS Brewer.

Sumara, D. (1996). *Private readings in public: Schooling the literary imagination*. Peter Lang.

Woolf, V. (1957). *A room of one's own*. Harcourt Brace Jovanovich. (Original work published 1929)

2 Inscape

William F. Pinar

"Aboutness," Mary Aswell Doll (2017) writes, "can only circumscribe the action, not tell the inside of the story" (p. 97). No "inside of the story" from me,[1] nor will I escape altogether circumscribing what Mary Aswell Doll has written in *The Mythopoetics of Currere*. I will aim for somewhere in-between the inside and outside, yes another citation-centered study[2] wherein from extensive quotation I attempt to reactivate Mary Aswell Doll's subjective presence as conveyed through concepts, specifically the concept of "inscape."

"Inscape" (Doll, 2017, p. 38) is "the unique inner nature of a person or object as shown in a work of art, especially a poem" (Merriam-Webster, n.d.).[3] Associated with Gerard Manley Hopkins—who derived it from the medieval philosopher Duns Scotus[4]—the concept denotes the expression of subjectivity in aesthetic, conceptual, and/or material form, establishing a through-line from the inner life[5] you affirm (dreams, emotion, thought) to the outer life in which you participate, teaching myth, fiction, and (inadvertently) curriculum theory.[6] The capacity—another key concept of yours to which I'll return later—to recognize the inscape of others Hopkins termed "instress," defined as (in Stephen Greenblatt's phrasing) "the apprehension of an object in an intense thrust of energy toward it that enables one to realize specific distinctiveness" ("Inscape and Instress," 2020). For Hopkins, "the instress of inscape leads one to Christ, for the individual identity of any object is the stamp of divine creation on it" ("Inscape and Instress," 2020).[7] While your teaching is not so aimed, analogous (if secular) concepts do surface in your text, concepts like "aura" (Doll, 2017, p. 68) and "shimmering Otherness" (p. 67). Your teaching is aimed at showing students how they can encode their "shimmering" even "soaring" subjectivity within their writing and other forms of art.[8]

"Rather than devote my writing class to topics such as animal rights or ecology," you tell us, "I have made the deliberate choice in this, my fifty-plus year as a teacher, to send my students on to their inward journeys" (Doll, 2017, p. 139). To do so, you ask students to "draw connections

DOI: 10.4324/9781003231547-3

between modern and ancient writing, back and forth continually, until time became more an ebb and flow than a line," then invited them "to tap time's flow within themselves by attending to their dream images" (p. 38). Dreams, "coursings from within" (p. 34), you characterize them, glimpses of one's own wild game,[9] appearing then disappearing into the woods, you in wide-eyed pursuit, life coursing through your veins. With these images and metaphors, I am reminded of Wittgenstein's ideal of a "primordial life, wild life striving to erupt into the open" (even though he rarely felt himself capable of it), an aspiration central, his biographer writes, "to understanding both the purpose of his work and the direction of his life" (Monk, 1990, p. 490). Would you say it is central to understanding yours a well?

"The main title of this book," you explain, "contains the word 'mythopoetics' to mean a metaphorical way to view curriculum" (Doll, 2017, p. xv). "Mythopoetics also implies literature," you continue, "a subject I have taught for fifty years" (p. xv), a "crone in the classroom" you claim (p. 142), telling us (as a wise old woman would) that "the teaching of literature can connect students . . . to what courses within them" (p. xv). "For my classes," you note, "myth and literature provide the avenue to self-study, if one is willing to take the plunge" (p. xvi).[10] I am reminded of the novel *The Lacuna* (Kingsolver, 2010), wherein Harrison Shepherd, the main character—"character is both It and I" (Doll, 2017, p. 139) you write—dives into lacunae, literal and metaphoric.[11]

You affirm the educational significance of fiction, its invitation to us to "live in language differently, more poetically, less literally," inhabiting worlds "both familiar and unfamiliar" (Doll, 2017, p. 50). How? "By studying short textual passages," you suggest, "students can experience the two-edged characteristic of fiction's unfamiliarity: its wonder, its risk" (p. 50). Studying short textual passages magnifies, like the blowup of a photograph. I recall Antonioni's 1966 movie *Blow Up*, wherein a photographer detects a murder when he magnifies a shot he's taken. Not always a crime of course, but often a telling detail does magnification reveal. You magnify (as you juxtapose[12]) space with time, recommending *adagio* not *allegro* as the rhythm of reading.[13] "Reading aloud slows," you note, "attending to punctuation slows. Time is a matter of attention, of attending, which is where all the varieties of instants grow" (p. 50).

To time and space you add "fluidity," noting that "fiction has a way of seeping," to and from the "soul," which, you suggest, it feeds (Doll, 2017, p. 51).[14] "In myth," you write, "opposite worlds blend together, need each other, act in tensive union; the cycle of life necessarily includes the underworld, and woman is not just a rib but a force of creation" (p. 58). Adam is dirt, "I am dirt" (p. 56) you assert, adding: "The dirt origin of Adam is Genesis' nod to early mythic and spiritual cosmogonies" (p. 57). As with Aboriginal cultures, "myths and stories were passed down orally though the use of the human voice and gesture and sometimes costume" (p. 60). Time amplifies and intensifies as it pauses: "To articulate the deeper resonances of subjectivity," you appreciate, "one must disengage from its flow by writing. This is like letters written in running water" (p. 62),[15] an Aboriginal-sounding phrase that is also the title of an earlier, equally memorable book (Doll, 2000).

You "teach to unlearn" (Doll, 2017, p. 121) you tell us, explaining: "The literatures I teach always teach me, prod me to think more deeply, appreciating the complications that come when givens are overturned. This is a constant process of unlearning, erasing one thing to make room for another" (p. 129).[16] For you that would seem to include unlearning the lessons of childhood.[17] "I am a child of the 40s and 50s and a daughter of the patriarchy" (p. 103), you tell us.

One man in your life was your brother, Duncan Aswell, who renamed himself Bill Cutler (Doll, 2017, p. 11), a brother who died too young, on May 16, 1988 (p. 15). He had settled in Atlanta with his husband, but you've always kept him close, even geographically, settling yourself, and your wife Marla, in Savannah. Close but perhaps ambivalently so, implied when you write, regarding your mother: "For all her rejection of gender stereotyping for herself, my mother's upbringing of me was very gendered. I was given dolls and taken to musicals. My brother was given books and taken to tragedies" (p. 23). In his early death, he was taken to tragedy.

That mother, your mother, was also the editor Mary Louise Aswell, her death acknowledged in the December 25, 1984 issue of *The New York Times*: "Mary Louise Aswell, an editor and writer, died yesterday in Santa Fe, N.M. She was 82 years old. Mrs. Aswell was the author of *Abigail*, a historical novel about Quaker life, and *Far to Go*, a suspense novel. She was editor of *It's a Woman's World*, an anthology of *Harper's Bazaar* stories, and served as an editor for *Harper's Bazaar* and for *Reader's Digest Condensed Books*. She is survived by a son, William Cutler of Atlanta; a daughter, Mary Doll of Fulton, N.Y., and a grandson" (Mary Louise Aswell, 1984). That grandson would be Will of course, now grown-up and married, you with grandsons, living (like your mother) in Manhattan. "Mother lived in New York City," you write, "apart from us, having left the marriage to our father four or so years after giving birth to me in 1940" (Doll, 2017, p. 17). New York is, you say, your "elsewhere," the city where "my mother surrounded herself with a literary crowd—adults she laughed with as I looked on" (p. 105). And away from the city too: you remember one "early summer" when your mother, brother Duncan, and you shared a house on Nantucket with Truman Capote (p. 18).

Mother and daughter "grew apart," you confide, until her illness brought the two of you together: "I tended her bedside, listened to her stories, fed her, and cared for her. I knitted her a pink afghan for her seventieth birthday and liked to wear her clothes, to mirror herself back to her. Then the tenderness returned" (Doll, 2017, p. 21). "After her death," you worked through your relationship with her through writing, publishing "Mother Matters: A Daughter's Hymn," composed, you say, by "a distant daughter," unfavored (you rue) but gifted (you appreciate) by the "exceptional experience she gave me, a kind of mothering that other mothers could never give" (p. 22). Now, with age yourself, you admit that you "feel closer to her . . . than I did when she was alive" (p. 23).[18] "[W]ho one's mother is matters," you remind, adding: "Yes, my mother will always be my m(other)" (p. 23).

That other man in your early life, your father—Edward Campbell Aswell—was, you say, "reserved . . . some say cold; but to me . . . playful" (Doll, 2017, p. 25). He was your "musical father" as he played the piano; he was, most famously, your literary father, editor to Richard Wright and Thomas Wolfe. Your father's death in 1958 shocked you so that you were "slow" to recover (p. 26).

Despite the mesmerizing nature of your parents' lives, from the outset, you were, you tell us, "already aware of the pull of the inner life" (Doll, 2017, p. xi). One of Jung's "formative ideas," you note, is "ghosts" (p. xi), and I suspect your parents and brother haunt you still. The second—"synchronicity," that "things happen and come together for a reason, which has nothing to do with the ego" (p. xii), reiterates reality as external, as mythic, as meaningful.

"What is it to write in the mythic mode?" you ask, answering: "It is to have the sense that trees breathe, the cosmos speaks, things change shape, and the world is essentially comedic, with a capital C, meaning that mythic writers write texts that show us the aliveness of life, including death" (Doll, 2017, p. 66). About death you write: "Death's power energizes life" (p. 71). For Eudora Welty—another writer your mother nurtured (p. 21)—death is "intertwined with life . . . mythic" and magical (p. 71). Like Aoki,[19] you reiterate: "we are humus; we are dirt, the skin of the earth" (p. 63). "All go unto one place; all are of the dust, and all turn to dust again," echoes Ecclesiastes (3:20 KJV).

"Texts that shock," you suggest, "are the best fictions to pull us away from the sentiment of sameness" (Doll, 2017, p. 141). One such text you teach is Kate Chopin's *The Awakening*, pointing out that "Edna Pontellier's rebellion was considered outrageous for her time and place, not only because she no longer subscribed to monogamy but, more, because she relished discovering the sensuality of her female skin" (p. 82). "The body has a mind of its own," you once remarked to me. That "body of knowledge," "bodied knowledge" you phrase it, informs your reading and your teaching (p. 81).

Besides Edward Albee[20]—whom you pronounce "a curriculum theorist extraordinaire" (Doll, 2017, p. 97)—you "nominate Ovid as a new darling of curriculum theorists," Ovid "that poet of the first century [who] wrote against the current of his time, preferring—instead of epics about men, conquest and adventure—tales of love and how love transforms. Upturning the Roman applecart, he forefronted women, desire, and interiority" (p. 73). You note that "in Ovid's work, no love is unnatural unless it arises out of a need for power and control" (p. 73), from which you move (as you ask your students to move from antiquity to modernity and back) to *Brokeback Mountain*, a "story of desire and duty and place" (p. 73). You cite the otherworldly nature of the mountain, "high above the tree line, its flowery meadows, and most symbolically its coursing, endless wind" (p. 75). You focus on that wind,[21] suggesting

> the action of the wind is nature's way of speaking to his [Ennis'] soul, trying to change his mind. The wind booms, strikes, courses, combs, bangs, and drives. There are no gentle zephyr breezes. According to ancient understanding, the soul is wind-like, related to breathe and vapor. To lack breath is to be without spirit; to be in the presence of spirit is to feel the wind.
>
> (p. 76)

You understand that "the issues of this novel and of the film based upon it are ever-present," pointing out that "Many of us choose to live our lives according to some outside force other than to the urgent call of the soul" (p. 76).

That call, once heard, requires, you continue—referencing Alice Walker—"to stand up, speak out, and get beside yourself" (Doll, 2017, p. 79).[22] That advice you take yourself, confessing "occasionally [I] act out and get beside myself" (p. 83). Costumes can help; maybe with Mardi Gras in mind you write that "masks bring out the hidden selves beneath the persona" (p. 79).[23] Like the curriculum, one's persona provides passage between inner and outer life, enabling subjective presence even through the enactment of scripts, making others' words one's own, coming alive in their enunciation. "Perhaps because this was theater," you write of Albee's *The Goat*, "live and on stage, I felt such an electric current" (p. 100). A coursing, one might say.[24]

"The function of art is to put us in contact with our possibilities" (Doll, 2017, p. 140) you admonish,[25] activating one's capacity to create.[26] "Capacity suggests wideness," you specify, "not narrowness; openness; space for possibilities not yet even imagined, or if imagined, done so with a tremble. . . . Instead, capacity holds room for unknowingness and peculiarity. Capacity is fearless in its embrace of the other inner side of things" (p. 96). There is the call, not only of your inner life, but that of others—inscape and instress—inviting not gossip (well, on occasion) but metaphor, "offering for those with eyes to see the under-layers of human action" (p. 98). And to read the portents human and non-human action can communicate.

To that end, you befriend the "monster," pointing to its etymology in French, "meaning to warn, to remind. The monster reminds of what is in danger of being forgotten, or puts us in a different mind, or puts us in a mind differently" (Doll, 2017, p. 100). You note that the Latin root is "monstrum," meaning "evil omen or portent," but you side with the French, affirming the monster's capacity to awaken us "to what lies below, slumbering" (p. 100).

"Allow my song/To sing the whirlwind" (Doll, 2017, p. ix) you write, introducing the book, an image that makes you a medium, a prism or passage through which reality—more mythic than empirical—moves, a coursing that denotes your attunement to what remains after the snow melts, uncovering the earthiness of experience, alive, moist, fecund, fantastic, a palimpsest of the psychic, itself, as you remind, "mythic" (p. xiii). "All moments assembled in a long row ahead of us/Like a line of seedlings Jeff had just planted/Giving us reason to think more westerly" (p. 9).[27] "Memory slides" (p. 30) you write; it is itself a slide, traversing time from now to then.

"November is my favorite month," you said,[28] staring past me out the dining room window onto the snow-covered ground, cocktail in hand. With that statement and that Mona Lisa smile you dissolved the dread[29] I always associated with that month while living in upstate New York, draped in its unending days of gray and cold. The snow was said to be a "lake effect," as if it were an afterthought of Lake Ontario, a rather long afterthought I should say, one that stayed long after November, often into April, when we were then deluged with one last sadistic snowstorm, at Easter on occasion, as if to bury us one last time before the promise of resurrection during the all-too-brief upstate New York summer. "Death and regeneration," you write, describing "goddess culture," the archaic past structuring the present (Doll, 2017, p. 136). Goddess culture meant, recalling the title of one of your mother's books, that *It's a Woman's World.*

You emphasize that "myth, above all, *is* metaphor" (Doll, 2017, p. 98). And so our little cocktail party—just the two of us, Bill Doll working on dinner in the kitchen—that gray November afternoon almost five decades ago recalls not only your dispelling of the gloom; it conveys your lifelong inspiration to me, your subjective presence contradicting the empirical present by an intoxicating transcendence of it, reactivating a mythic past where death almost disappears into regeneration. Like Medea and Anne Sexton,[30] you too are a woman of excess, exceeding what is, inscaping a landscape, a classroom, a text, an ongoing accomplishment you make seem simple, you self-knowing sly one. You know (recalling the opening line) the "inside story." "[W]hat matters most," you know, "is understanding the self—personally, historically, politically[31]—so as to place subjectivity as the cornerstone of education, and then to take that education into the world" (p. 143). That, Mary Aswell Doll, you have done.

Notes

Author's Note: An earlier version of this chapter was first published as Pinar, W. F. (2020) "Inscape", *Journal of the American Association for the Advancement of Curriculum Studies*, 14(1). The author is grateful to the Co-Editors at JAAACS, Susan Mayer and Patrick Roberts, for their invitation to publish the original essay.

1. Except for one scene near the end, nothing here—dear Mary—from "inside" our forty-six-year-old friendship, except a familiarity of address, as (except in the sentence in the text to which this endnote is appended), I address you directly.
2. A citation-centered study enacts my conception of curriculum as complicated conversation, an invocation of orality as the voice of the person cited becomes almost audible, reactivating a sense of subjective presence. The scholarship of the curriculum theorist—the composition of synoptic texts specifically—documents "a citation-centered existence" (Fishbane quoted in Pinar, 2019, p. 377; see also Pinar, 2006).
3. "Inner life," you remind, "is, after all, of a poetic nature, which is why dreams (our inner fictions) are such a central stage for the playing out of our real-life drama. . . . Dreams lie a little, making us work to see the meaning in the lie" (Doll, 2017, p. 140). So does "real life" lie, positioning us as sleuths at both ends.
4. John Duns (1266–1308), commonly called Duns Scotus, was a Scottish Catholic priest and Franciscan friar, university professor, philosopher, and theologian. He is one of the three most important philosopher-theologians of Western Europe in the High Middle Ages, together with Thomas Aquinas and William of Ockham ("Inscape and Instress," 2020). Perhaps the term is derived from "within scape," scape denoting "a long, leafless flower stalk coming directly from a root," here a metaphoric not literal idea. Interestingly—a side note to be sure—Walter Benjamin saw in Scotus' thought a precursor to his own philosophy of language; he planned to rationalize his postdoctoral dissertation research with reference to Scotus, what Eilenberger (2020) judges to be a "stroke of brilliance" (p. 91). The problem was that someone else already had the idea, and [had] executed in 1915 as a postdoctoral dissertation. As luck would have it, the scholar in question was Benjamin's former peer and soon-to-be fierce rival at Freiburg, Martin Heidegger. Benjamin was informed about Heidegger's work by [his friend Gershom] Scholem in February 1920. "I knew nothing about Heidegger's book," Benjamin admitted in his reply to Scholem in December 1920 after months of silence, then continued: "I have read Heidegger's book about Duns Scotus. . . . The author' abject sycophancy towards Rickert and Husserl does not make reading it any more agreeable. In this book Duns Scotus' philosophy of language goes largely unexamined, so no task is accomplished" (pp. 92–93).
   Your invocation of Scotus' idea, Mary, is likewise a "stroke of brilliance."
5. Affirming the inner life can be an ethical move, ethics conceived not as rules or social norms but an enactment of personal integrity, "attunement" to what is

just in each situation (Pinar, 2019, pp. 263, 268, 281). This elusive idea is one that has moved many, among them Ludwig Wittgenstein, who, Monk (1990) explains, was influenced by the idea provided by Arthur Schopenhauer and Karl Kraus (the great *fin de siècle* Viennese satirist) "that what happens in the 'outside' world is less important than the existential, 'internal' question of 'what one is'" (p. 19). You (or I) would not so prioritize—you (and I) testify to their reciprocal relationship—in our time the inner seems sometimes eclipsed by the "outside" world. In that sense, *currere* is a corrective.

6. "Now, you may ask, what does all this myth, memory and dream stuff have to do with curriculum? My answer is Everything" (Doll, 2017, p. xiv).

7. I am reminded of the icon, not an image on a computer screen but its medieval antecedent, the phenomenology of which Steimatsky (2008) specifies: "The rhetoric of the icon—which, like the relic, claims to provide visual, material evidence for the incarnation of the sacred in the world—asserts Christianity's redemptive vision of God's materialization in Jesus. The iconic image is not simply 'symbolic' or 'allegorical' in relation to its divine referent, as it would be in a Protestant system that severs the manifest and the hidden, the flesh and the spirit. Rather, it is grasped as participating in what it represents: it is an index of Christ's humanity; in partaking of his body it incarnates God" (pp. 138–139).

8. "My students rise above the text," you tell us, "but they do not soar" (Doll, 2017, p. 69). That you do, and not only in this text but in each of your distinctive stunning studies: 1988, 1995, 2000.

9. Encoded in curriculum, the "wild game" of inner life become tamed, attuned to terms at once self-expressive and communicative, elements of the unconscious recoded as concepts explained in public. "The unconscious is a poetic not a scientific reality," you know (Doll, 2017, p. 38).

10. "For inspiration and an understanding of irrational truth," Watson (1989) notes, "Pasolini [too] turned to myth" (p. 12).

11. One is an underwater cave where he swims seeking psychological (re)birth. "Often," you write, "caves are considered the wombs of the Earth" (Doll, 2017, p. 115).

12. A key curriculum concept, juxtaposition, Strong-Wilson (2021) explains, is "a mode of bringing disparate things, people, events into provocative relation, even these also remain distinct from one another" (p. 23).

13. "It is good to read much," Ciardi and Williams (1975) allow, adding: "It is even more important to read a little in greater depth" (p. 6)

14. "Gender," you note, "rather than being fixed, is a fluid notion like water" (Doll, 2017, p. 132).

15. Such disengagement seems a form of non-coincidence: Pinar (2019, p. 17).

16. In her essay on domestic life in early modern England, Dabhoiwala (2020, March 26) suggests that "The universal impulse to customize everyday space can be seen even in cave dwellings, prison cells, and office cubicles" (p. 54). When you "make room" are you also "customizing," modifying (something) to suit a particular individual or task, modifying meaning as inscaping (if I may make a gerund out of a noun)?

17. Unlearning one's childhood—implied in your remembrance of your own childhood's patriarchal character—alters one's sense of being-in-the world, recalling the reciprocal nature of subjective and social reconstruction. "Through this 'unlearning,'" Wendy Kohi (1993) notes, "and through an examination of the structural preconditions that accompany such unlearning, those of us committed

to social transformation may be better equipped to create a new politics, a politics of 'difference' that acknowledges multiple forms of political agency" (p. 127). While that era allowed that more optimistic outlook, even in our own—living in the catastrophe of COVID-19 amplified by the incompetence and corruption of the Trump administration—"resolve" can sustain us (Pinar, 2015, p. 80).

18. Your acknowledgment allows me to confide that with age, I also feel closer to my mother, my own marvelous Malinda.

19. "Wisdom," Aoki (1993/2005) tells us, "is inscribed in a family of words: human, humility, humus, and humor, all etymologically related" (p. 213).

20. Discussing a performance of Albee's *The Goat*, you make the curriculum theory connection clear: "Albee's drama, if it is pathological, is full of pathos: it confronts issues of love, identity, capacity, interiority, and shame" (Doll, 2017, p. 101). The title of the play reminds me of Pasolini's *Porcile*. My favorite Albee is *Who's Afraid of Virginia Woolf?*, especially film version.

21. What Harold Bloom (2019) termed "the ancient praxis of poets innumerable" (p. 366). A few pages later, he quotes from Archie Randolph Ammons' poem *Guide*; this line seems in sync with your insight: "the wind was gone and there was no more knowledge then" (p. 369).

22. Besides noncoincidence, for example, being in-between inner and outer worlds, being beside oneself might also invite "inscaping," encoding one's subjectivity in material form, as you ask your students to do when you ask them to write as a form of self-study.

23. Once again, the meaning is in the lie, the phrase you associate with dream interpretation, as earlier noted.

24. Coursing is an intensification of live(d) experience, what Jerzy Grotowski sought (his book is *Towards a Poor Theatre*, a title we modified for our own *Toward a Poor Curriculum*), what provided *currere* with its "theatrical methodology" (Grumet, 1976/2015, p. 88). "In practice," Madeleine Grumet explains, "*currere* has projected itself into the world in the forms of autobiography and theater," adding: "Autobiography and theatre are art forms and, as such, are symbols for human experience and feeling that are particular and specific rather than general and abstract. *Currere*, focusing upon the educational experience of the individual student, finds within autobiography and the theater appropriate symbols for that experience, for both autobiography and theatre are forms of self-revelation" (p. 88).

25. I use that verb because it seems to me you are (implicitly) criticizing those who regard art's function as only entertainment or distraction; beauty, as you imply, acts like an icon, religious art that lifts us out of ourselves, besides ourselves (as you note), to partake in what lies beyond, the mythic perhaps, and the spiritual, intertwining concepts in your *oeuvre*.

26. I am reminded of George Grant's November 6, 1942, journal entry: "Art is wonderful—it is part of all—it is the beauty that gets us nearer to the final and ultimate reality, but the reality of living is greater, nobler than the art itself. The depth of one's own feeling is deeper than any art one could produce. . . . It is because the medium, however well it is used . . . still it is a medium—& not the person" (quoted in Pinar, 2019, p. 86, n. 216). You are suggesting the two are interrelated, that person reconstructs herself through aesthetic, including literary, forms, as she expresses herself through them: inscape.

27. As I prepare this for publication—it is a cool bright blue-sky morning in the Pacific Northwest, the morning of July 24, 2021—and my husband Jeff is

outside watering his "seedlings," now grown tall, all in summer bloom, an abundance of beauty reminding me of our—you, Marla, Jeff, and I—many times together, including that early evening at your New Orleans home on State Street Drive, chatting over cocktails, seated in your backyard, watching enormous yes monstrous rats skirt across the electric lines, their own I-10 interstate highway.

28. This scene occurred in your Fulton, New York, home, not long after we met, so perhaps in 1977, during November of course.
29. "Winter is there, outside, is here in me": a line from Conrad Aiken, a native of Savannah, now your town too (quoted in Bloom, 2019, p. 390).
30. "Like Medea, Anne Sexton was a woman of excess," you note (Doll, 2017, p. 117).
31. "Just improve yourself," Wittgenstein would later say to many of his friends, "that is all you can do to improve the world" (quoted in Monk, 1990, pp. 17–18). "Political questions, for him, would always be secondary to questions of personal integrity" (Monk, 1990, p. 18).

References

Aoki, T. T. (2005). Legitimating lived curriculum: Towards a curricular landscape of multiplicity In W. F. Pinar & R. L. Irwin (Eds.), *Curriculum in a new key: The collected works of Ted T. Aoki* (pp. 199–215). Lawrence Erlbaum. (Original work published 1993)

Bloom, H. (2019). *Possessed by memory: The inward light of criticism*. Alfred A. Knopf.

Ciardi, J., & Williams, M. (1975). *How does a poem mean?* (2nd ed.). Houghton Mifflin Co.

Dabhoiwala, F. (2020, March 26). Bed, bench & beyond. *The New York Review of Books*, 54–55.

Doll, M. A. (1988). *Beckett and myth*. Syracuse University Press.

Doll, M. A. (1995). *To the lighthouse and back*. Peter Lang.

Doll, M. A. (2000). *Like letters in running water: A mythopoetics of curriculum*. Lawrence Erlbaum Publishers.

Doll, M. A. (2017). *The mythopoetics of currere. Memories, dreams, and literary texts as teaching avenues to self-study*. Routledge.

Eilenberger, W. (2020). *Time of the magicians. Wittgenstein, Benjamin, Cassirer, Heidegger, and the decade that reinvented philosophy*. Penguin.

Grumet, M. R. (2015). Toward a poor curriculum. In W. F. Pinar & M. R. Grumet (Eds.), *Toward a poor curriculum* (pp. 84–112). Educator's International Press. (Original work published 1976)

Inscape and instress. (2020, March 5). In *Wikipedia*. https://en.wikipedia.org/w/index.php?title=Inscape_and_instress&oldid=901535313

Kingsolver, B. (2010). *The lacuna*. Harper Perennial.

Kohli, W. (1993). Raymond Williams, affective ideology, and counter-hegemonic practices. In D. L. Dworkin & L. G. Roman (Eds.), *Views beyond the border country: Raymond Williams and cultural politics* (pp. 115–132). Routledge.

Mary Louise Aswell Obituary. (1984, December 25). *The New York Times*, 18.

Merriam-Webster. (n.d.). Inscape. In *Merriam-Webster.com Dictionary*. Retrieved March 5, 2020, from www.merriam-webster.com/dictionary/inscape

Monk, R. (1990). *Ludwig Wittgenstein. The duty of genius*. Penguin.

Pinar, W. F. (2006). *The synoptic text today and other essays: Curriculum development after the reconceptualization*. Peter Lang.

Pinar, W. F. (2015). *Educational experience as lived: Knowledge, history, alterity*. Routledge.

Pinar, W. F. (2019). *Moving images of eternity: George Grant's critique of time, teaching, and technology*. University of Ottawa Press.

Steimatsky, N. (2008). *Italian locations: Reinhabiting the past in postwar cinema*. University of Minnesota Press.

Strong-Wilson, T. (2021). *Teachers' ethical self-encounters with counter-stories in the classroom. From implicated to concerned subjects*. Routledge.

Watson, W. V. (1989). *Pier Paolo Pasolini and the theatre of the word*. UMI Research Press.

3 Reflections on a Mythopoetics of Listening for a More-Than-Human World

Marilyn Hillarious

In the introductory chapter of *The Mythopoetics of Currere: Memories, Dreams and Literary Texts as Teaching Avenues to Self-Study*, Mary Aswell Doll (2017) frames her mythopoetic study of self and world through two ideas gathered from her reading of Carl Jung's autobiography. The first is the idea of "ghosts" or "hauntings" that intrude unannounced—within dream, memory, or cultural fantasy—bringing one's internal, subjective world into relational and productive tension with an external, historical, and sometimes obscure lifeworld. The second is the idea of synchronicity. Channeling Jungian thinking, Doll writes, "Things happen and come together for a reason, which has nothing whatsoever to do with the ego," and yet, as subjective beings, we find meaning in these synchronicities; assuming such coincidences must be of significance to our lives—significance to be acknowledged, interpreted, and understood (p. xii). For Doll, these Jungian ideas, provide vital cues toward mythopoetic inquiry and *currere*. In her words, the "shimmering Otherness" (p. 67) of ghosts, synchronicities, or a surreal world help interrupt the otherwise static reverie of a too rationally perceived world, and reveal instead something of the world's "two-ness"— its "right and left, conscious and unconscious" depths (p. 6). Through the myth of Odin's sacrificial (and rational) eye, Doll explains that in this sense of two-ness, "we are being re-minded to observe our worlds with greater imagination but also to re-turn to the buried (repressed, forgotten) contents with greater insight" (p. 6).

In this paper, taking a cue from Doll, I employ literature to guide me through the mist of synchronicities and hauntings that emerged as I read her book. Doll's book prompted my own *currere* via mythopoetics and deepened my engagement with literary texts, as I sought to untangle intervening and interweaving threads of myth and memory. Pursuing that disentanglement in this paper, I hope to break through the doldrum of "chiseled belief systems" (Doll, 2017, p. 49) and "deadened imaginations" (p. 50) to instead recover a "wider dimension of selfhood" (p. xi) more attuned to this world's

DOI: 10.4324/9781003231547-4

two-ness and, as such, to "that which courses within" (pp. xv, 49). Strictly speaking, when I was first asked to write a response to Doll's book, I had just finished reading Richard Powers' (2018a) *The Overstory*. In this melancholic, yet radically hopeful novel, myth plays a not-so-small role, surfacing both the subjective and intersubjective lives of trees and human beings. Set primarily in the 1980s and 1990s, at around the time of the Timber Wars in the Pacific Northwest,[1] this mythic tale of human and nonhuman American lives affords an imaginative entry into an understanding of environmental relationality, where at stake is not just the survival of old-growth forests and their biodiversity but also, importantly, the meanings we ascribe to *being* in this world filled with other living things. Coming on the heels of my reading of *The Overstory*, Doll's *Mythopoetics of Currere* seemed to offer a crucial response to this particular time in our lives—one marked by climate change and rising global temperatures, widespread forest fires, the Covid-19 pandemic, and increasing global resistance to economic and social precarity.

In one of my favorite lines in the book, Doll (2017) writes "myths are psychic stories, the psyche is mythic" (p. xiii). With this, she conveys something primal about the stories we tell of humanity, and of our primal origins, not to mention the uncanny, elusive, yet yawning force of the unconscious that is always at play within the myths we tell about our more-than-human world. Following Jungian depth psychology, Doll suggests that myths take shape through and provide us with the psychic archetypes of our sometimes poetic, sometimes romantic, but always already "ancestral" fantasies of self in relation to others and the world (p. xi). Contrasting Jung's "nonstandard" mythopoetics to Freud's "standard" scientific approach to the psyche, Doll notes that Jung's focus on myth and archetype allows the unconscious to be apprehended as "a living foreign entity within us," one we might only correspond with "in an 'as if' manner," either poetically or metaphorically, and not as "a thing" of scientific reality (p. 38). The poetic presence of the unconscious also suggests that meaning, in myth and fairytales, is "never overt but rather a beckoning 'something' we need to address" (p. 139). To that end, myths, she says, "are not meant to teach" or instill a particular morality as maybe fables do: "No, myths open our portals to what lies beyond, beside or below the surface" (p. 66). Through her engagement with dream, memory, and literary fiction, Doll's mythopoetics of *currere* wrests the study of the human psyche out of the scientific realm and situates it within the humanities, making available to us an astounding postmodern, feminist, even postcolonial critique of the hegemony of Western, Eurocentric perspectives on modern subjectivity, while also turning our attention toward the *something* we must address if we are to engage in ethical relations with self, other, and the world.

Understanding the psyche as mythic, rather than scientific, is helpful to me as a scholar interested in the *mythologies* about educational technology (and technology in general) within neoliberal educational spaces. Since early 2020, as Covid-19 forced the shift to teaching and learning online across the world, I have grown especially concerned about the opportunity this presents to further entrench educational spaces within discourses of efficiency, productivity, and accountability that circulate profusely within the realm of education technology. Such discourse not only disavows and exacerbates widespread inequity in access, quality, and inclusivity across class, race, gender, and disability divides but also provides the seductive, mythic structures that help guide the psyche toward disciplinary self-surveillance and market-oriented techno-rationality, undermining both social relations and historical memory in the process. In this essay, I seek to follow in Doll's (2017) footsteps by inviting extended critique to the problem of modern subjectivity that she articulates—a critique that pulses with and interrogates those ruins of the past and fantasies of the future that are woven into the architecture of modern life. Further, I explore the significance of Doll's mythopoetics of *currere* in terms of what it offers our imaginative capacities when faced with the devastation of modernity's techno-rationality. In doing so, I rely on the foundational work of curriculum theorists: William Pinar, Madeleine Grumet, Peter Taubman, and Mary Doll herself to draw attention to how technology transforms educational experience into "technostructure" (Pinar, 2012, p. 173) and to further emphasize *currere* as a reparative means to recover what is "lost from ourselves" and from our education (Pinar, 1976/2006, as cited in Doll, 2017, p. 139).

Following that, I draw on writings of novelists and cultural critics, Amitav Ghosh and Richard Powers, both of whom I had read prior to Doll (2017) and who, coincidentally, engage with myth and the imagination in ways that help extend and build upon my understanding of Doll's mythopoetics. I examine Amitav Ghosh's (2016) *The Great Derangement: Climate Change and The Unthinkable* in conjunction with Doll in order to unfold a critique of modern subjectivity, shaped across time and space, and, in particular, through history and fiction, wherein the combined logic of scientific instrumentalism, globalized capitalist production, and white supremacy undermine our ability to imagine environmentally and socially just relations among all living things in this world. Further, I also elaborate on my engagement with Powers' (2018a) deployment of themes of myth, time, and stillness within *The Overstory* in order to highlight a theory of mythopoetic listening—key to both Doll's and Powers' writing—as a vital means to engage in imaginative alterity with an external, historical, mostly obscure lifeworld, so that "worlds without can become worlds within" (Doll, 2017, p. 139). In the final section, I synthesize these arguments to demonstrate Doll's mythopoetics of *currere* as a mode of recognition and a politics of responsibility for a more-than-human world, wherein psychic movement between self and society works to counter the kind of literalist thinking engendered through a system of disciplinary, techno-capitalist rationality within the modern society.

Doll's (2017) articulation of *currere* rooted in mythopoetic engagement with the unconscious sets itself apart from and in intriguing tension with modernity's educational project, where universal standards of industrialization and informatization have turned students and teachers into data, curriculum into bytes of digital information and test scores, and literacy into rampant "literalism" (p. 49). For Doll, literalisms signify closure, a collapse in meaning-making, as the imagination is stifled and understanding occluded in favor of *chiseled belief systems*. She suggests that literalism is baked into the current standardized testing and accountability regime, fueled, for example, by textbooks that fail to disturb sedimented assumptions and by knowledge coded as information, arranged into "neat columns" and "packages" and forgotten "once the test has been taken" (p. 49). She also warns that literalist thinking foments ignorance because devoid of imagination, such thinking can lead to hate, bigotry, and violence. Literalisms, she says "make us ill" because they comprise "modern myths without the metaphors" (p. 49). Absent the imagination or betraying "deadened" (p. 50) ones, literalisms force us into a "state of constant hunger" (p. 52) for an emotional life we are forced to disavow, thus depriving us of the subjective resources necessary to be responsible for a world under siege. Doll's literalisms bring to mind Taubman's (2009) description of the Lacanian term "quilting points" (p. 106), which under normal conditions present as necessary illusions for psychic stability: "points along the signifying chain where the signifier is attached to the signified, at least momentarily" (Oxford Reference, 2022). However, Taubman's (2009) central concern is that, through the impact of neoliberal education reform, some educational terms, such as "standards" and "accountability," which usually have loose and heterogenous meanings and are "always potentially contestable and subject to rearticulation and redeployment," have instead become fixed and stabilized. He argues these quilting points recode embedded racism and class structure within school systems as manageable *not* through systemic solutions such as "combating racism or class inequities or the excesses of the market" but through redirection toward a biopolitics of disciplinary practices, governmentality, and audit culture that enforces corrective action upon the individual (pp. 106–107). The latter is at the heart of the process of restructuring subjectivity within school systems, where those of us in education "disappear into 'best practices' that sustain our omnipotence, provoke our sense of emptiness, and hystericize us as we turn more and more to . . . the gaze of the big Other to tell us who we are and how we are doing" (p. 48). In other words, both Taubman and Doll warn of the destructive effect of increasing rigidity in language and meaning in schools today, which—failing investments in imagination or insight—secures the psyche to dangerous and reductive fantasies, including that fantasy of freedom from dependency on others and the world.

Doll's (2017) engagement with mythopoetics is rooted in psychoanalytic examination of premodern, modern, and postmodern texts, whether juxtaposed alongside dream, memory, or historical account. This juxtaposition of texts from personal to public and also in relation to the text's status relative to *modernity* is propelled by Doll's critique of the "modernist mindset," which she argues cannot tolerate complexity, chaos, or paradox, the density of language, and, specifically, otherness (p. 88). Modernity is often associated with the period of Enlightenment in Europe, when science was substituted for religion "as the governing mythology of life" (Pinar, 2015, p. 114). Scientific reason—fueled by the desire to order, classify, explain, control, and predict—determinedly turned toward instrumental rationality and certitude to create a modern world ostensibly free from mythological belief, religion, and human submission to the vicissitudes of natural world. In reality, this obsessive turn arguably facilitated a regression into religious belief in "the authority of science, and the exactitude of numbers" (Taubman, 2009, p. 7). Via the work of Walter Benjamin, Gilloch (1996) suggests that tyrannical belief in scientific reason in truth marks the "reversal or inversion of this human submission to nature in the modern period" (p. 10). He notes that these fantasies of liberation from nature as a result of technological progress and scientific instrumentalism accompany a particular disciplinary reality: "unchanging rhythms of the machinery [human beings] must serve" in order to access and maintain bourgeois life. The result is an "intensification of myth" in modern life (p. 11). In other words, myths of technological control merely provide the illusion of freedom from—and control of—nature even as it chains us to the machinery of capitalist production and commodity fetishism.

From this point of view, fantasies of or mythological belief in technocratic and scientific power work to colonize the modern techno-capitalist imagination, rendering public things like the natural world or our educational system into a business of numbers, where all living and nonliving things are appropriated into capital, becoming either consumer or consumed. In the world of online learning, disciplinary technologies of self-regulation and market-oriented techno-rationality engender further entrenchment within this "technostructure" (Pinar, 2012, p. 173). Following Arthur Kroker's (1984) critique of technology's effect on subjectivity, Pinar (2012) argues that the "world" *becomes* "technostructure," or the " 'lens' through which we perceive the world" when technology, working like disease, affects us "not from outside, but from within," blurring psychic "distinctions between inside and outside" in an environment that has become "a technological 'extension' of the human body and our senses" (p. 173). Human experience slowly, subliminally becomes "merged" with technostructure (p. 173), overtaken by anxiety as "time itself flatlines, as the past and the future disappear into an endless present" (p. 174). In the online context, or cyberspace, with its instantaneous and anxious "anytime, anywhere" type of educational experience, our subjectivities disperse into "sensory immediacy" (p. xvii), giving birth to "a minimal or narcissistic self" that fantasizes either about remaking "the world in its own image or [merging] into its environment in blissful union" (p. 142). In the face of such dangerous fantasies and against the backdrop of climate change, Doll's mythopoetics of *currere* offers us instead the opportunity to engage in an ongoing mode for ethical recovery of oneself and one's educational experience.

Following William Pinar and Madeleine Grumet's (1976/2006) foundational work on *currere*, Doll (2017) employs free associative engagement with memory, dreams, myth, fairy tales, and fiction to invite "something" (pp. 126, 128) primal, forgotten, repressed, or otherwise deferred back into language and into "complicated conversations" with her lived experience of the world (Pinar et al., 1995, as cited in Doll, 2017, p. 47). In other words, supported by the notion of curriculum as complicated conversation and through her engagement with mythopoetics, Doll extends the alterity of *currere* to include a more-than-human world. According to Pinar (2012), *currere* is a necessary process that facilitates "private passages into the public world" (p. 44). He notes that while "private can imply isolation from historical forces and social movements," *currere* engages the public intellectual in self-reflexive understanding and social reconstruction through academic study of "the sources of interiority and the provocations of theorizing and teaching" that arise from historical consciousness (p. 32). He also notes that just as subjectivity experiences and translates the work of history and society, it can also sometimes speak for the natural world. Following Paul Wapner (2010), he suggests, "[O]ur thoughts, fantasies, and constructions are not self-originating but instead develop in relationship to the more-than-human world of which they participate" (Wapner, 2010, p. 209 as cited in Pinar, 2012, p. 33). Without such engagement in internal academic study, in relation to a more-than-human world, the public intellectual risks engaging in the "unmediated expression of emotion projected onto the social surface" in a misrecognition of their own interiority as "the world" (p. 33). For Doll (2017), it is the reciprocity between myth and psyche and her recognition of it within the practice of *currere* that makes way for subjective inquiry into humanist and/or post-humanist discourses as well as personal and cultural mythos. Through poetic recovery of unconscious, emotional content, she disturbs literalist readings and opens up her imagination to alterity and allegory.

By way of his critique of modern literary canon, Ghosh (2016), like Doll (2017), is concerned about modernity's effect on the human capacity to imagine otherwise, specifically in light of problems posed by growing environmental crisis and forced migration. Central to his argument is the failure of the modern novel to help shape cultural imagination on climate change.

He contends that the contemporary literary novel, as part of the historical moment within which it was born, valorizes rational, emancipatory motifs and makes the turn inward just as modernity itself turned toward commodity fetishism. Accordingly, realist fiction has presumed the earth to be a source of unlimited resources, which helps permit and sustain a belief in "the regularity of bourgeois life" (p. 75) while relegating the uncanny presence of the dehumanized or nonhuman other to the "outhouses" of fiction: i.e., fantasy, science fiction, or horror (p. 40). Via Franco Moretti (2006), he suggests that the novel takes its modern form through the "relocation of the unheard-of toward the background . . . while the everyday moves into the foreground" (Ghosh, 2016, p. 31). This move, he argues, acts as concealment, making it particularly difficult for the modern novel, with its narrow conceptions of time and space, "to recognize . . . the challenges that climate change poses" (p. 16). Describing these novels like "modern myths" (Doll, 2017, p. 49), he writes that they derive out of "something broader and older . . . from the grid of literary forms and conventions that came to shape the narrative imagination in precisely that period when the accumulation of carbon in the atmosphere was rewriting the destiny of the earth" (pp. 16–17). In other words, Ghosh describes our particular epoch's cultural embrace of modernity's project through the guise of the modern novel as exceptionally devastating. Undertaken during the "Great Acceleration,"[2] the embrace of modernity limited cultural imagination to a bourgeois capitalist imaginary while simultaneously disavowing its effect on the environment and poor and vulnerable communities around the world (Ghosh, 2016, p. 131). Like Doll (2017), Ghosh calls for a fiction, history, and politics conceived of differently, inclusive of both human and nonhuman others, that makes it possible "to approach the world in a subjunctive mode, to conceive of it *as if* it were other than it is" in order to imagine other "possibilities" (p. 156).

In turning toward a mythic unconscious and examining the strange metaphors that surface within memories, dreams, and ancient and contemporary texts, Doll's (2017) mythopoetics of *currere* recovers "*something* of our premodern legacy as we move inevitably into the age of becoming cyborg" (*my emphasis*, Bosnak, 2000, p. 203, as cited in Doll, 2017, p. xiv). Drawing on Fleener (2005), Doll explains, "the as-if logic of poetry and metaphor offers a different way to comprehend the mysteries of the planet," depending "not on the rational mind but on the creative, imagining mind revealed in stories, myths, and metaphors of human-cosmic interrelationships" (p. 90). Additionally, the return to premodern myth and its internal poetic logic, she notes, unearths a vague, forgotten *something*— "a slight disturbance" (p. 143) or a "shimmering Otherness" (p. 67)—within educational experience that encourages intersubjective negotiation and a capacity to imagine differently, especially necessary as we struggle to work through the belief systems that have led to our own dehumanization and the destruction of our environment. In other words, for Doll, myth and metaphor provoke a mythopoetic recognition of the world's *two-ness* and, as such, our relationality with life in all its forms in this more than human world. Doll's *currere* brings to mind Biesta's (2010) notion of educational responsibility in the modern world is, where responsibility is "first and foremost a [moral] responsibility for a particular, 'worldly' quality of the spaces and places in which 'newcomers' can come into presence" (p. 91). Here, Biesta surfaces the political character of Arendtian notions of plurality, natality, and difference[3] within the idea of a *worldly* educational experience—experience that invites uncanny encounters with alterity, thus allowing for the appearance of *newcomers* in a process of subjective reconstruction. Understanding Doll (2017), by way of Biesta's notion of educational responsibility, conveys a sense of her underlying political stance in these "too-literal times" (p. 101). Specifically, Doll's *currere* is a compelling call for mythopoetics within the public realm of political action, wherein one can undertake educational responsibility for a world in which human, nonhuman, or even "hybrid" newcomers come into presence (p. xiv).

We meet many *newcomer* others as we follow the delicate thread that weaves its way through the labyrinth of Doll's (2017) mythopoetic and deeply autobiographical curriculum inquiry. In early chapters from Section One, *Dreams and the Curriculum of the Remembered Self*, she describes memories of her mother, father, and brother, working through memory, myth, and metaphor to reveal the specter of familial otherness. In ensuing chapters, Doll explores mythical archetypes within her dreams to do battle with the formidable demands placed upon her gender and sexuality by the "monsters" ingrained within patriarchy (p. 34). Further on, in chapters across Section Two, *The Mythopoetics of Currere in Literary Texts*, she confronts "the Great Chain of Being" (p. 56)—via its imposition of modern Western Eurocentric discourses of the body and knowledge, human nature and identity, culture, race, and nationality, and gender and sexuality—unearthing the "rich deviations" within our ancient and modern literary texts that "draw on fantasy and imagination" so as to reveal alterity and allegory in relation to a more than human world (p. 38). Thus, we follow the unconscious into metaphors of a subterranean and "chthonic female" darkness (p. 23) or read it in the alterity provoked by human desire for, rejection of, or transformations into nonhuman (turtle, snake, pig, tree) or superhuman (Innana, Athena, Medea, Pan) entities within diverse mythic folklore. For Doll, this mythopoetic relationality is an acknowledgment of "a posthuman world, where humans connect psychically with [nonhuman life]; reminding further that we are all hybrids within our own species" (p. xiv). *Newcomers* are thusly brought to bear through images and metaphors that loosen the unconscious and "inspire psychic movement" (p. 140) between language and memory, dream and desire, and academic study and public life. Reading texts written in the "mythic mode" (p. 71), Doll notes, engenders such psychic movement by putting us in touch with "our possibilities" (p. 140)—the uncanny, outer limits of what we might be able imagine—while at once enabling the kind of distance necessary to encounter the strangeness within.

When Doll (2017) describes writing in the mythic mode, she might well be speaking of my experience of Richard Powers' *The Overstory*. She muses,

> It is to have the sense that trees breathe, the cosmos speaks, things change shape . . . mythic writers write texts that show us the aliveness of life, including death. Texts are full of hardship, color, shape, sound, love in multiples and diversities. There is the sense that all things rise and fall, wind and circle back, always with verbal awareness, -ing in motion. Humans, animals, plants, stones interact, as do deities with humans, plants, animals, and stones. Writers in mythic mode reveal profuse con-fusion
>
> (p. 66).

For Doll, both ancient and modern writers are at play here. From Ovid to Flannery O'Connor and Eudora Welty, they all write to jolt the reader's imagination out of sedimented, "pious," or otherwise literalist thinking (p. 66). In O'Connor's work, she finds that "the surreal world of nature is a key mythic aspect . . . [suggesting] that there is another reality surrounding the human realm which contains its own intentions" (p. 67). There are surreal echoes of exactly this within *The Overstory*, where the lives of trees—usually relegated to the backdrop of human stories—are foregrounded alongside nine human protagonists, who invest in these trees a life full of rich meaning. In the book, the trees (and societies of trees) that we are introduced to—from pine and maple, to elm, fig, and chestnut, to mulberry, oak, linden, and more—are treated as narrative subjects, who come alive through the use of metaphor and myth and are imbued with agency and intentionality. The trees speak to us and to each other; they live in communities; they protect and mourn lost relatives; they migrate; they draw microorganisms, animals, and human beings alike into doing their bidding; they remember the past, record memory, and predict the future.

Powers' (2018a) *The Overstory* also arrives almost *as-if* in response to Ghosh's (2016) call for mythopoetic fiction; a kind of fiction that might address "the lost objects" of our cultural imagination (Lertzman, 2015). In researching responses to this novel, I encountered many reviews of the book that found it hard to put into words how *The Overstory* affected them—only that it had changed their view of the world in some vital way. Lertzman's (2015) research,[4] borrowing from the work of Christopher Bollas (1987/1991), suggests that this may be because an engagement with lost objects of environmental devastation induces what she calls "environmental melancholia" (p. 4)—a state where "environmental damage and loss" cannot be mourned because symbolizing it requires acknowledging an internalized environmental object, one too devastating to encounter as damaged. Environmental melancholia functions, therefore, through a more "generalized guilt," even a "collective form of paralysis," and complex "ideological defensive structures, such as equating environmental practices with being non-capitalist and 'un-American'" (p. 127). In other words, our melancholic response to environmental loss may be tied to an inability to reconcile a simultaneous investment in the very forces—unfettered capitalism, nationalism, and/or American exceptionalism—that, in part, cause these losses. That being said, such ambivalence, Lertzman asserts, can also be a vast resource for creative engagement with one's feelings of loss. Doll (2017) agrees. She suggests that experiences of ambivalence with fiction written in the mythic mode facilitate an "opening out in a situation of estrangement that affirms life's possibilities" (Doll, 2017, p. 101). Following Georges Bataille (1991), Doll argues that it is through estrangement and the "rupture of structures" that one is finally able to see in an "*ex orbitant*" manner: to "what knowledge is hiding . . . to see outside the orb, so as to view the metaphor that hides inside the plot" (p. 101).

Powers (2018a) organizes his book into the four sections of a tree: Roots, Trunk, Crown, and Seeds, providing a macroscopic "tree metaphor" for the microscopic human activities that unfold within each section (Masiero, 2020, p. 138). In other words, the novel as "tree" provides a holding space for the human stories contained within it. In fact, the synoptic mode of storytelling allows Powers to "collapse distinctions between natural history and human history," furthering the impact of the comparatively longer lifetime of trees on the story's mythopoetics and sharpening that sense of mutuality between human-nonhuman lives (Chakrabarty, 2009, p. 201). In this way, the book resonates with Doll's (2017) notion of time from a mythical standpoint, where "to view time mythically is to honor the eternity of the present moment, where there is no past or future" (p. 60). In other words, the past and the future are always, already implicated within an eternal present and, therefore, yoked to one's responsibility for a time yet to come.

Further, the structure of the *The Overstory* also facilitates mythological or, as one critic, Masiero (2020), suggests, "biblical form," where readers (and nine human protagonists) are taken on a journey from "partial and imperfect knowledge" about the lives of trees to "new truths that the parable has revealed" (p. 138). Resonating with the Bible, the "Roots" section begins with a prologue that intones, "First there was nothing. Then there was everything. Then, in a park above a western city after dusk, the air is raining messages. A woman sits on the ground, leaning against a pine" (Powers, 2018a, p. 6). The unnamed woman, who we later learn is Mimi

Ma, one of the protagonists of the novel, "listens, tuning down her ears '*to the lowest frequencies*'" (Masiero, 2020, p. 140) to hear the pine tree speak to her in "words before words" (Powers, 2018a, p. 6). This is how we come to understand that the pine tree is the narrator of the story that follows, amounting to "the literal manifestation of Powers' desire to give voice to trees" (Masiero, 2020, p. 141). Strangely, it is also one of the very few places in the book where a tree actually speaks, even as one understands by the end of the novel that the tree has always been speaking.

As it were, Powers (2018a) uses structure and form to organize the reader's experience of the book as a mythic journey, while also facilitating a perceptual shift—right at the start of the book—to an uncanny "third space" (Hongyu Wang, as cited in Pinar, 2011, p. 107), where a temporal sense of a "double encounter—alterity in the other and other in oneself" permits the kind of psychic movement that makes way for subjective and potential social transformation (p. 107). In other words, through the novel's structure as well as the use of mythopoetic literary devices, Powers' (2018b) is able to foreground a sense of "listening" as central to the temporal condition of *being* in a world with others, one that necessitates becoming attentive to "meaning above and beyond our own" (n.p.). As Doll (2017) reminds us, this is the work of all artists who work in mythic mode—they who bring forth a "vast depth quality, . . . [a] capacity, of interiority"—to provide the space that holds together meanings of our own making alongside those we imagine are beyond our own (p. 99). For Powers (2018a), and a growing mass of writers, Ghosh (2016) included, this mythic mode is intended to infuse the cultural imagination with new mythologies that challenge modernity's emphasis on anthropocentrism, human exceptionalism and autonomy. Likewise, the mythopoetic significance of *The Overstory* serves to reinforce Doll's project, where the *as-if* logic of poetry, myth, and metaphor make way for imaginative meaning-making in relation to our conscious and unconscious attachments to nonhuman entities, like trees, thus diverging from an epistemological orientation that privileges the interiority of human beings *alone* as a source of meaning in the world.

Both Doll's (2017) and Powers' (2018a, 2018b) writing are deeply influenced by Ovid—in particular, by his stories of metamorphoses and the role it can play in disturbing both the written and unwritten rules of society. In *The Overstory*, all of the characters "turn into other things" (Powers, 2018a). Trauma, disability, illness, and incarceration deepen and transform multiple protagonists' relationship to both time and, as well, to a world lived in with *other* living things. In particular, Powers (2018a) suggests themes of "stillness" accompanied by attentive "listening" as what facilitates this capacious engagement with time and a more-than-human world. In one example, two protagonists from the novel, Ray and Dorothy Brinkman, whose lives are traced from "meet-cute" to marriage, and then from infertility to affair and near-divorce, suddenly find themselves tied together by tragedy when Ray suffers a stroke. Ray's transformation from an able-bodied individual to a vulnerable invalid is first cast as misfortune, as they both find themselves "buried" (Powers, 2018a, pp. 390, 441) under the full weight of his illness. But Ray's enforced *stillness* allows first him, then both of them, to pay attention to the growing transformation of their backyard from domesticated garden to untamed wilderness. Specifically, as Ray begins to adjust to his immobility and marvels at the growth of a small chestnut seedling—a metaphorical stand-in for the daughter they never had—Dorothy begins to see Ray anew: "His years of enforced tranquility, the patience of his slowed mind, the expansion of his blinkered senses. He can watch the dozen bare trees in the backyard for hours and see *something* intricate and surprising, sufficient to his desires" (*my emphasis*, p. 478). Dorothy moves past her own desires—"a hunger that rushes past everything" (p. 478)—to join Ray in watchful stillness, as their garden becomes a space where their shared fantasies of a child metamorphize into a garden grown wild. Their stillness reminds me of Doll's (2017) close reading of the Eudora Welty (1979) story, *Livvie*, where Doll notes how "stillness enhances the room, becoming a gathering spot" for the ceaseless movement of desire, enlivening the imagination to see, hear, and feel *something* anew (p. 71). For Dorothy and Ray, the *something* that comes into presence are the many trees they have planted in their garden over the years. They decide to "do nothing" (p. 480), opening their doors to these "strangers" in their midst (p. 478). Over time, a wilderness grows untamed, bringing with it a surge in insect and animal life, threatening the sensibilities of the neighbors in the upscale suburb in which they live. This results in the once benign tide of psychic capaciousness in Dorothy rising to civil disobedience when first the neighborhood and then the city call for their backyard to come to order once more. Here, Powers' writing powerfully suggests the inevitability of the rule of law. Nevertheless, this seems to be nothing compared to the near 70-year-old Dorothy's "second growth," a capacious aliveness that invades her being as she thinks, "Here I am, near the finish line, loving life again" (p. 488).

Ray and Dorothy's story mirrors what Doll (2017) describes as the point of Ovid's stories of metamorphoses, in that they are attempts to question the way the law "interferes with," "ruins," or represses the fullness of life (p. 73). The distinctiveness of Ovid's stories, she insists, is that they disturb order, instead forefronting "movement, change, and transformation as psychic necessities" (p. 76). Drawing inspiration from Ovid, Powers (2018a) too is interested in disturbing the order of things. At a point late in his story but before his stroke, Ray Brinkman reads Christopher Stone's (1972) seminal treatise: *Should Trees have Standing? Law, Morality, and the Environment*. It prompts him to think against the Kantian ethic: "as far as nonhumans are concerned, we have no direct duties. All exists merely as means to an end. That end is man"

(p. 271). For Ray, it is a crisis come to a head and a reminder of the absurdity of Kantian rationalism. Ray is a patent and property rights lawyer. He knows his marriage is cracking at the precipice of his beliefs regarding ownership and the protection of capital versus Dorothy's indefatigable desire for her own freedom. Later, ruminating on his choice of career in the wake of his stillness, he comes to believe that he has been part of one of the longest "war crime[s]" in history (p. 270)—a war crime defined by an enduring legacy of Kantian misrecognition of the (political) rights and freedoms accorded to dehumanized and/or nonhuman others. Through Ray (and Dorothy), Powers' (2018a) demonstrates the transformative power of psychic movement, the Ovidian understanding that "people turn into other things" (p. 134). Ray and Dorothy, Powers signals, are like Ovid's Baucis and Philemon, "two immortals who came to Earth in disguise to cleanse the sickened world," "opening their door to strangers," and rewarded for their efforts by living past death "as trees—an oak and a linden—huge and gracious and intertwined" (pp. 516–517). For Powers, trees provide a fundamental metaphor for stillness and metamorphosis: like the seeds of a tree, each person must germinate: some "swallowed, etched in digestive acid, expelled as waste" and others "smashed open" before they turn into something else (p. 518). Or put another way, like a seed, "a thing can travel everywhere, just by holding still" (pp. 6, 518).

If myths are psychic stories, then *The Overstory* as myth repeatedly deploys a motif of *stillness*, one rooted in the temporality of subjectivity, while attuned to tree and historical consciousness, in order to, as Doll (2017) might say, de-literalize the mundane and bankrupt stories we construct about the world and make them new again. In an interview, Powers (2018b) expands on the theme of stillness, suggesting that

> to hold still is to shift postures from dominant to accommodating, to trade use and mastery for looking and receiving. And when a person holds still and looks, all the agents and emissaries of the meaning out there begin to look back and start talking.
>
> (n.p.)

For Powers (2018a), as with Doll, stillness conveys a mode of *being* that involves attentive and embodied listening. Each character, in their stillness, is able to attune themselves to a slower, greener (tree time) frequency, where newcomers can be heard and their presence once again felt. For Doll, as noted earlier, stillness provides *a gathering spot* for the flow of desire, where time slows down and one can begin to "have a sense that trees breathe, the cosmos speaks, things change shape" (p. 66). In Eudora Welty's stories, Doll finds that stillness anticipates mystery and chaos in the world, it's "shimmering Otherness" (p. 67), which helps illuminate in and recover from chaos a sense of *something* uncanny, old, or forgotten (Doll, 2017, pp. 70–71). In the modern world, mystery and chaos are "kept mum" (Michel Serres, as cited in Doll, p. 59), time accelerated, and darkness banished as the fact of our own mortality is buried under a "glassy bright" (p. 49) system of classification, domination, and mastery. In this world, where "logos, not eros rules" (p. 56) and literalisms indeed prevail, an attunement toward stillness and listening, within our fictions, our bodies, our histories, or our politics, is an opening out or a harkening toward the embodied and erotic unconscious, which circulates between, within, against, or in excess of the words in play. Doll calls to mind the Sumerian myth of Innana, responsible for the growth of plants and animals, who descends to the underworld by setting "her mind to the Great below" (Wolkstein and Kramer, 1983, as cited in Doll, 2017, p. 90). Mind implies hearing, Doll notes, and in the primal, unknowing darkness of the underworld "ear, not eye, takes precedence," allowing "upperworld" rationality to be informed by an underworld "unconsciousness" (p. 90). In other words, as in the darkness, in stillness too we listen, and through this listening we open up the potential to tap into the coursing within.

In her book, Doll (2017) draws us into a mythopoetics of *currere* that points the way toward new geographies of listening, where the grammar of being alive, of being human within the constraints of our modern mythologies, can be put to the test by what comes out of the dark—when we stop to listen. Where mythopoetic writing may function to decenter the mythos of human exceptionalism and, as well, our perception of time and autonomy, without *currere*, myths too can descend into literalist readings. Doll notes that "mythic stories (particularly) are very dark, providing the opportunity to explore the unknown. But without proper probing students simply gasp and turn the page. We must dwell a while in the dark" (p. xv). Thus she cautions that "we must come to know the threads that lead us back to the uncovering of our monsters, lest we thrust them [back] out onto the world" (p. xiii). This dwelling in the dark, or in 'stillness,' helped me pay close attention to feelings of "environmental melancholia" (Lertzman, 2015, p. 127) that my reading provoked. I sought to enter a place where it was possible to register and unpack the uncanny absences and ruptures in this narrative. Drawing on Pinar (2012), Doll reminds us that for *currere*, it is the "double movement between study and self-study" that offers the capacity for transformation and social reconceptualization (p. 139).

For me, this is why "place" comes to be yet another character in the polyphony of voices within *The Overstory*. Via Jean Shinoda Bolen (1992), Doll (2017) suggests, "'When humans are the main characters in any scene, the location is on land' (p. 230), meaning that Place is the formation of character" (p. 142). In this sense, *The Overstory* is a distinctly American novel featuring seven white Americans and two second-generation Americans, one of Indian and another of Chinese descent. It is a polyphonic story about time and trees, but one set in a country built upon modernity's tenets, specifically that of private property, and in tension with American myths[5] regarding immigration and identity tied to the land. Tracing the influence of Eurocentric religious and cultural beliefs all the way from The Book of Genesis to the philosophical underpinnings of Descartes and Kant, Doll critiques the construction of the American or Euro-Western mindset, wherein values rooted in the "Great Chain of Being" (p. 56)—in other words, a "linear, sequential order" (p. 56), the "fact" of *man's* "hierarchy" over woman and nature, and an "overriding message" of "dominion, obedience, punishment, and debasement"—facilitate a "tidy" account of the world, grounded in an elevation of Western European white male epistemologies related to appropriation and control (p. 57). Drawing on Tim Dean (1991), Casemore (2008), too, describes "a theory of American culture that takes the land to be the primary figure of American unconscious," one which discloses the hegemonic construction of the "American subject" in the figure of the white male colonial settler, "who, in confluence with nature and in pursuit of a mastery of consciousness over nature, translates his subjectivity into poetic discourse" (p. 69). This poetic construction of the "American subject," Casemore explains, simultaneously obfuscates a history of relations with the land, where it "became the material site of deracination and genocide of American Indians" while providing the source of "symbolic identification" for European Americans, one divorced from "the nation's violent history" (p. 69). In other words, poetic articulation, or the mythic ideation, of the North American landscape is the site from which emerges an American consciousness that relies on the unconscious (and conscious) erasure of histories of racist, sexist, and anthropocentric white heteropatriarchies that continue to make a "hegemonic American subject" possible (p. 69).

In this regard, how Powers' (2018a) articulates the "American subject" of his novel, and its historical and present-day relations with the land, becomes meaningful: There are no Native American, African American, or Latinx protagonists in *The Overstory*. Instead, the two non-white protagonists are from minority communities usually chosen to demonstrate uncomplicated model minority discourses and therefore easily subsumed into hegemonic narratives of American identity—especially, in its transfiguration into the modern neoliberal subject. Curiously, as can be seen in the Brinkman's story, Powers' does occasionally take up and contend with the historicity and interdependency of issues related to class, race, gender, and disability within his mythopoetic understanding of the American landscape. Still, I came to deeply feel the *shimmering* absence of *othered* American perspectives in his story. The omission creates a profound void within Powers' mythic ecological story, and it deepened my sense of melancholia about the ways in which narratives about our current ecological crisis are frequently disconnected from or, in some cases, purposefully blind to narratives of historical and sociopolitical injustices with which they are deeply intertwined.[6] We see it in the way the Black Lives Matter movement plays out in parallel with the ongoing pandemic, where connections between neoliberal policies, state violence, poverty, health, and rollbacks on environmental and social protections in African American and/or in other poor and vulnerable communities are deeply felt. According to Key Stone Pipeline protestors, similar issues are manifesting due to the proposed expansion of the pipeline, which runs through Indigenous land and is causing both food and water contamination as well as increased cases of sexual violence and Covid-19 due to an influx of oil-industry migrant labor. Doll (2017) reminds us that melancholia provides the impetus for an imaginative return to the "murky" depths of the self in relation to context and history, where the "self opens out to . . . one's personal story that joins its mythic pasts" (p. xii). Following her cue, I find myself asking, what is my responsibility to self, other, and the world, when my relationship to place is itself metaphorical, my subjectivity enmeshed with globalized neoliberal and technocratic systems of thought, and I become one of the many who might read the novel too literally, as simply an ode to trees and their would-be saviors.

Reading *The Overstory*, a mythopoetic narrative about trees set within our ongoing climate crisis, surfaced my own ancestral "ghosts" and "hauntings." It made me think of my grandfather's journey to Malaysia to find work on a British colonial rubber-tree plantation just before the Second World War; my parents' journey to Kuwait—a country that is largely desert, and increasingly so after two Gulf Wars—to find work during the height of oil discovery in the Middle East; my own journey as a nonresident alien first in Kuwait and then in the United States under the growing umbrella of a global war on terror. When Doll (2017) writes of Asian American poet Shirley Geok-lin Lim's (1996, 1998) narratives of otherness—across self, gender, family, place, and culture—she speaks to these ghostly hauntings of mine. Lim's autobiography and her poetry capture the story of a family that migrates repeatedly across the globe and across generations, shapeshifting along the way, in search of work, home, place, and identity. Doll refers to Lim's narrative as a poetics of "Elsewhere" (p. 106)—a poetics tied up with feelings of shame, loss, regret, and nostalgia that surface in relation to her negotiations of place and identity. These Elsewhere poetics recall my own sense of place—a liminal relation between alienation and belonging—that is more common than ever among routinely isolated, globalized, and cosmopolitan working class or among a more precarious class of workers who are *forced* to migrate for work or due to war and/ or environmental appropriation or devastation. In this sense, the otherness of Elsewhere threatens to become the norm for most human beings on Earth.

For me, the story of our climate crisis is inextricable from the mostly invisible, globalized system of extractive and financial capitalism, and the generational flow of cheap human labor required to support it, especially during the 70-year period of the *Great Acceleration*. From earlier, more visible, colonial forms of oppression, exploitation, and industrial pollution, modern technology has helped make complete the shift toward near-invisible neocolonial technologies of global capitalism and neoliberal technologies of self in a process that Nixon (2011) calls "slow violence" (p. 2).[7] Existential concerns in our modern world, such as climate change and environmental devastation as well as historical injustices, that are still socio-economically and politically relevant to the same people who are often precariously susceptible to environmental crisis, manifest too slowly and imperceptibly within the "violent geographies of fast capitalism" (Watts, 2000, as cited in Nixon, 2011, pp. 7–8). "Out of sight," "gradual," and "dispersed across space and time," the concept of slow violence reinforces Doll's (2017) mythopoetic sense of time *and* space, as yet beyond our comprehension and thus rendered inexplicable to the modern imagination (Nixon, 2011, p. 2). As techno-capitalism and globalization shear off our clear-eyed view of self and world, literalist thinking dominates and our capacity to imagine the world differently is slowly and tragically diminished.

In such space, where vision is so obscured as to become unreliable, Doll's (2017) mythopoetics of *currere* orients instead toward deeper mythopoetic listening—one where we might excavate and bring to the fore the inextricable connections between and/or disavowals of human and nonhuman others within our fictions, our politics, or our histories. Through her *currere*, Doll revives myth—via indigenous, ancestral, modern, and postmodern stories—and through it a mythopoetic sense of time and place, wherein *something* old and forgotten or new and uncanny works to disturb a world made too-literal. What surfaces in Doll's pedagogy here is the sense that it isn't that we don't have enough information or facts at our disposal to live ethically in this world full of other living things, but that we are unable to remember, pay attention to, or imagine differently even with the information we do have. In this paper, prompted by Doll's *currere*, I explore mythopoetic fiction through Powers' *The Overstory* in an attempt to bring together an epistemology of *being* and living ethically with others in this more-than-human world. Doll (2017) and Powers' (2018a) work *as if* in sync to produce a theory of mythopoetic listening that allows me to think about place and identity differently; that is, through a prism of environmental, spatial, and intersubjective relationality, wherein the fact of our dependency on others—even, or especially, in online educational contexts—cannot be avoided. Even if, like seeds, we are isolated, scattered, and germinating apart from each other, we might—in the time we take to be still within our educational spaces—allow ourselves to listen, with play and possibility, to others who are *always already* a part of our educational commons.[8] In this sense of listening, Doll and Powers echo Low et al.'s (2017) theory of psychoanalytic listening, where relations of listening in a "public sphere [can act as a] keepers of the commons" (p. 86). Mythopoetic stories of migration, social and environmental justice movements, environmental loss, or stories of our collective and transformative power that inevitably intersect with stories of inter-species and interspatial connection offer a reparative and generative "third space" (Wang, as cited in Pinar, 2011, p. 107), wherein listening invites a capacious reciprocity with others. Doll's pedagogy reminds us of the power of following our unconscious through memory, dreams, and literature, making it possible, in this current moment, to interrogate the modern myths to which we may be too deeply affiliated. Conversely, psychic inquiry into our mythic investments may also unearth how "we are all hybrids within our own species" (Doll, 2017, p. xiv). In the stillness we have wrought within this spatiotemporal moment, we may be able, as Doll urges us, to take the time to do the necessary work of sorting through our melancholia in order to imagine new possibilities and allow newcomers into our shared, democratic, and educational commons.

Notes

1. The Timber Wars or the Redwood Timber Wars refers to an evolving period in American history, starting first in the 1990s when scientists, conservationists, and activists squared off against logging companies in Humboldt County, California, to protect the last remaining old growth forests and locally endangered biodiversity. Specifically, environmentalists fought legal battles to save the Northern Spotted Owl because of the presence of laws to protect wildlife rather than ecosystems in the United States at the time. The northern spotted owl thus worked as a stand-in for the old-growth forests in the area. Bipartisan legislation, such as the Endangered Species Act, continues to be challenged by timber companies as well as by locals, whose lives have been decimated due to the socio-economic fallout from the banning logging.
2. The Great Acceleration is a term coined by John R. McNeill and Peter Engelke to refer to the 70-year period of recent human history, where three-quarters of the atmosphere was loaded with human-caused carbon dioxide. Citing McNeill and Engelke (2014), Thomas, et al. (2016) note that "the number of motor vehicles rose from 40 million to 850 million; the number of human beings tripled to about 7.4 billion; 1 million tons of plastic became 300 million tons; 4 million tons of synthesized nitrogen (mainly for fertilizers) rose to more than 85 million; the levels of methane and phosphorus are unprecedented in the experience of our species. And on and on. These changes are not merely taxing ecosystems; they are transforming those processes irrevocably" (p. 931).
3. In *The Human Condition,* Arendt (1958) is concerned about bringing thinking (*vita contemplativa*) back into the domain of action (*vita activa*), and through it, enlivening political intent and civic life. She worried that, in the modern world, thinking, a process of dialoging with oneself and (thus) creating consciousness and conscience, was becoming a solitary activity and, hence, becoming separated from the domain of political action. In Arendtian terms, "vita activa" or "human life in so far as it is activity engaged in doing something" is composed of labor, work, and action (Arendt, 1958, pp. 7, 22). Plurality, she notes, is "a condition of human action" because "nobody is ever the same as anyone else who ever lived, lives, or will live" (p. 8). According to her, this condition of difference is also embedded in the fact of natality. She notes, "the new beginning inherent in birth can make itself felt in the world only because the newcomer possesses the capacity of beginning something anew, that is, of acting. In this sense of initiative, an element of action, and therefore of natality, is inherent in all human activities" (p. 9). It is action, she argues, grounded in the fact of its own natality, and pursued within the Cartesian scientific tradition of the modern world, that has suffered most from both, the absence of contemplative thought, and the disappearance of political intent (pp. 9,

14, 304). For Arendt, contemplative thought troubles action, and vice versa, and it is through this disturbance, and the fact of natality, that Arendt hopes political action becomes meaningful and the mortality of men eludes its own end (p. 19).

4. Lertzman (2015) uses a framework of psychosocial research to explore people's ongoing engagement with ecological crisis within their communities near the Great Lakes in the Green Bay area of Wisconsin.

5. Samuels (1999) describes the period after American industrialization in the 1800s, when Americans were trying to establish a national culture against the backdrop of European mythmaking. At the time, agrarian farming was increasingly giving way to extractive industries and a "newly enlarged mercantile class," with diverse identities and affiliations, who depended on natural resources such as trees for their fortunes. Laying waste to these natural resources had the effect of producing a longing for an idealized past, insensible to the racialized and gendered order that made this past possible. European Americans answered the call for a mythic American consciousness by glorifying a culture "rooted in the soil," and thus to the land (p. 9). In other words, American consciousness and pride grew around the living monuments, such as the ancient trees of the Pacific Northwest, Yosemite, Niagara Falls, etc., which increasingly began to provide points of "mythic and national unity" (p. 9). Similarly, Hardt and Negri (2000) point out the role of the "open space of the frontier" in creating an American imaginary tied to "unbounded territory" that is "open to the desire of humanity" (p. 168). This idealization of the land, of course, obscured the system that was 19th-century American capitalism: "an ecology-gobbling, territory-colonizing machine fueled by slave accumulation, genocidal Indian removal, patriarchal family socialization, corporate paternalism, labor exploitation, universal education, and a Protestant calling to Manifest Destiny" (Widick, 2009, p. 22).

6. There is a long history of racism and exclusion within the environmental movement. Starting with John Muir, the founder of the Sierra Club, the environmental movement often attaches, what Nixon (2011) calls, an "exclusionary ethics of place" that involves a kind of "spatial amnesia" (p. 239). That is, environmental writing often includes an expansive allusion to, yet is also accompanied by amnesia about, non-American geographies that are implicated, through "legacies of war or outsize consumerism," within an American sense of place (p. 239). These environmental writings—for example, those of John Muir, Edward Abbey, Mary Austin, etc.—are particularly hostile to "dispensable, anonymous, invisible inhabitants who reside" or depend on the land in question or in a "world beyond" (p. 239). Furthermore, these writings frequently argue for political solutions related to land grabs, population control, anti-immigrant policing, militarized borders, setting carbon limits in the Global South, etc. (Ghosh, 2016). We see such policies take effect in, for example, the "Green Colonialism," of Zionist factions in Israel, where environmentalist discourse offered opportunities for "land grabbing and occupation" (Klein, 2016, p. 1). Likewise, Klein (2016) also describes the "long, painful history in the Americas" of discourses of the wilderness leading to them "being turned into conservation parks," preventing, in the process, "Indigenous people from accessing ancestral territories" (p. 2). The environmentalist movement, itself, has long been dominated by mostly rich, Western nations and NGOs, wherein the "environmentalism of the poor" and/or voices from Global South are frequently excluded, minimized, or disappeared into the background (Nixon, 2011).

7. Nixon (2011) describes slow violence as "violence that occurs gradually and out of sight, a violence of delayed destruction that is dispersed across time and space, an attritional violence that is typically not viewed as violence at all" (p. 2). In the context of neocolonial globalization and environmental devastation, recognition

and making visible forms of slow violence bring to the fore long-term casualties and, in turn, resistant action to such incremental violence.

8. For Low et al. (2017), education is a common good, meant to engender "affiliation with communities rather than promoting the rights of the individual" (p. 10). As such, educational experiences offer a fertile ground for relations of listening to be cultivated so as to remake human relationships outside of existing institutional structures and mediate a "new democratic body of the commons" into being (p. viii).

References

Arendt, H. (1958). *The human condition* (2nd ed.). University of Chicago Press.

Bataille, G. (1991). *Inner experience*. State University of New York Press.

Biesta, G. J. J. (2010). *Good education in an age of measurement: Ethics, politics, democracy*. Routledge.

Bolen, J.S. (1992). *Ring of power: The abandoned child, the authoritarian father, and the disempowered feminine*. HarperCollins.

Bollas, C. (1991). *The shadow of the object: Psychoanalysis of the unthought known*. Free Association Books. (Original work published 1987)

Bosnak, R. (2000). Jung and technology. In D. P. Slattery & L. Corbett (Eds.) *Psychology at the threshold: Selected papers from the proceedings of the international conference at University of California, Santa Barbara* (pp. 177–189). Pacifica Graduate Institute Publications.

Casemore, M. B. (2008). *The autobiographical demand of place: Curriculum inquiry in the American south*. Peter Lang Publishing.

Chakrabarty, D. (2009). The climate of history: Four themes. *Critical Inquiry, 35*(2), pp. 197–222.

Dean, T. (1991). *Gary Snyder and the American unconscious: Inhabiting the ground*. St. Martin's Press.

Doll, M. A. (2017). *The mythopoetics of currere: Memories, dreams, and literary texts as teaching avenues to self-study*. Routledge.

Fleener, J. M. (2005). Introduction: Setting up the conversation. In W. E. Doll, Jr., J. M. Fleener, D. Trueit, J. St. Julien (Eds.), Chaos, complexity, curriculum, and culture: A conversation (pp. 1–20). Peter Lang.

Ghosh, A. (2016). *The great derangement: Climate change and the unthinkable*. Apple Books, Penguin Group (USA) Inc.

Gilloch, G. (1996). *Myth and metropolis: Walter Benjamin and the city*. Blackwell Publishers Inc.

Hardt, M., & Negri, A. (2000). *Empire*. Harvard University Press.

Klein, N. (2016). Let them drown: The violence of othering in a warming world. *LRB, 38*(11), pp. 1–9.

Kroker, A. (1984). *Technology and the Canadian mind: Innis/McLuhan/Grant*. New World Perspectives.

Lertzman, R. (2015). *Environmental melancholia: Psychoanalytic dimensions of engagement*. Routledge.

Lim, S. G. L. (1996). *Among the white moon faces: An Asian-American memoir of homelands*. The Feminist Press at the City University of New York.

Lim, S. G. L. (1998). *What the fortune teller didn't say*. West End Press/University of New Mexico Press.

Low, B., Brushwood Rose, C., & Salvio, P. M. (2017). *Community-based media pedagogies: Relational practices of listening in the commons.* Routledge.

Masiero, P. (2020). The tree is saying things in words before words: Form as theme in Richard Powers' the overstory. *DEP*, *41*, pp. 135–150.

McNeill, J. R., & Engelke, P. (2014). *The great acceleration: An environmental history of the anthropocene since 1945.* The Belknap Press of Harvard University Press.

Moretti, F. (2006). *Serious century: From Vermeer to Austen. In F. Moretti (Ed.) The novel, volume 1: History, geography, and culture* (pp. 364–400). Princeton University Press.

Nixon, R. (2011). *Slow violence and the environmentalism of the poor.* Harvard University Press.

Pinar, W. F. (2011). *The character of curriculum studies: Bildung, currere, and the recurring question of the subject.* Palgrave Macmillan.

Pinar, W. F. (2012). *What is curriculum theory?* (2nd ed.). Taylor & Francis Group.

Pinar, W. F. (2015). *Educational experience as lived: Knowledge, history, alterity. The selected works of William F. Pinar.* Routledge.

Pinar, W. F., & Grumet, M. (2006). *Toward a poor curriculum.* Educator's International Press. (Original work published 1976)

Pinar, W. F., Reynolds, W. M., Slattery, P., & Taubman, P. M. (1995). *Understanding curriculum: An introduction to the study of historical and contemporary curriculum discourses.* Peter Lang.

Powers, R. (2018a). *The Overstory.* Apple Books, W. W. Norton & Company.

Powers, R. (2018b, April 7). Here's to unsuicide: An interview with Richard Powers. Interview with Everett Hammer. *Los Angeles Review of Books.* https://lareviewofbooks.org/article/heres-to-unsuicide-an-interview-with-richard-powers/

Oxford Reference. (2022). *Quilting Point.* www.oxfordreference.com/view/10.1093/oi/authority.20110803100359484

Samuels, G. B. (1999). *Enduring roots: Encounters with trees, history, and the American landscape.* Rutgers University Press.

Stone, C. (1972). *Should trees have standing? Law, morality, and the environment.* Oxford University Press.

Taubman, P. M. (2009). *Teaching by numbers: Deconstructing the discourse of standards and accountability in education.* Routledge.

Thomas, J. A., Parthasarathi, P., Linrothe, R., Fan, F. T., Pomeranz, K., & Ghosh, A. (2016). JAS roundtable on Amitav Ghosh, The great derangement: Climate change and the unthinkable. *The Journal of Asian Studies*, *75*(4), pp. 929–955.

Wapner, P. (2010). *Living through the end of nature.* MIT Press.

Watts, M. J. (2000). *Struggles over geography: Violence, freedom, and development at the millennium.* Hettner Lectures No. 3. Department of Geography, University of Heidelberg.

Welty, E. (1979). *Thirteen stories* (R. M. Vande Kieft, Ed.). Harcourt Brace Jovanovich.

Widick, R. (2009). *Trouble in the forest: California's redwood timber wars.* University of Minnesota Press.

Wolkstein, D., & Kramer, S. (1983). *Inanna: Queen of heaven and earth: Her stories and hymns from Sumer.* New York: Harper & Row.

4   Conjuring Spirit, Incarnating Soul in Curriculum Study

Molly Quinn

New Orleans at Dusk

New Orleans at dusk, along St. Charles Avenue
The day softly departs,
In gentlemanly, or perhaps gracious belle, fashion,
Gives easy way to eve
Though, oh, so slowly, a sweet Southern drawl—
Crisp, fresh, cool and bright;
Full-on spring delight comes night—
As I stroll the boulevard sidewalk.

A receiving line of azalea vividly greets and welcomes me:
"Good Evening," they whisper a cappella,
in pinks, timid and deep, brilliant and burgeoning,
Accompanied with angel white lights,
luring me on to my Italianate sanctuary,
the Columns Hotel.

The red berry hymnals here there are as well,
Standing tall and erect in their season's song;
Hope proclaims and 'pops' eternal
In ornamented chorus, both expressive and subtle,
All beside and before this festival, fiesta, of green
Arching over, embracing, me and my path—
The true Mardi Gras crowd, participants all.

They witness my presence, even celebrate it;
They themselves testify that
all things hidden shall be revealed;
When all seems lost, life, even love, returns—

DOI: 10.4324/9781003231547-5

And, in fact, at the last hour, after it:
unimaginable possibility, surprising benevolence,
universal and natural law.

The great old live oaks,
Their stance, one cannot ignore;
Ancient lore they tell,
And more recent—as beads hang
whimsically from their branches.

When night falls,
Their twisted bramblings
Command all attention,
Well lit;
Moonlight, stars, street lamplight, car headlights—
All fade.

The bell tolls . . .
From the Cathedral tower,
Keeping vigil before these mighty trees.
And I notice the flags hanging
From this grand old porch—
New Orleans, Louisiana, the U.S. of A.
I am again filled with doubt.

History mostly hurts.
Humanity rarely heals.
Can nature really speak
to human affairs?

But, you say, "You are sipping
on wine, over fried green tomatoes
and crab cake in remoulade sauce,
on the porch of the Columns Hotel."

Ah, too true, with the offerings
my father gave me for this right—
Eternal Patriarch, to whom I bow.

The power, too, of suggestion,
And love to a friend;
You dearly asked this very thing I attend—

I write just something, this way,
our woes perhaps to mend.

Earlier we lay on green clover
In a park, water's edge,
Before art museum, sculpture garden,
a paddleboat, kayaking friends.
This oak above held grand chimes
that rang lovingly in the soft wind.

We wondered how life had flown by,
And we flying with it—no, flown by it too,
The hopes for such moments
And many more such as this
Unrealized and untaken.

If flight, though perhaps not, weighty
We, rather compelled and consumed
By the work and way of the Big Apple
And its bite.

Later you showed me this secret garden
You had found.
Beneath quirky lights strung
upon ripe foliage and trees
Well-placed welcoming bird seductions
and pleasantly colorful, capricious chimes
The Little Easy. Rhapsody in Green.

Sitting before couples sprawled out upon
The grassy knoll—amid canoodle picnics and naps
And solitary poets sinking into their texts
We too enjoyed our bench and coffee talk
Me with my cup and you with your cake,
Bright garden paraphernalia and graciously
appointed chess-nook also in view.

"How do they live like this?"
"How do they find the time?"
We imagine this the everydayness
of life here in the languid, slow, easy city,
and fill ourselves with longing.

Is not this the home too, though,
Of profound compulsion and consumption?
A city set on the shores of decadence,
and carried by the wakes of indulgence?
And amid oh so many commanding
watery graves and wailing ghosts
too that speak.

Maybe that's it, then.
The body here as the phoenix rises up
In a kind of protest born by the sign
of nature's resilient hope, and perpetual return.

Emboldened, this embodied creole care courts
Not the unending march of progress—
The soft sciences of sensuality its sustaining
Underbelly understandings,
Rooted revelations.

Its knowledge, life, and way of being
rather in the tucked-away and
unexpected treasures and pleasures
To be found in a hidden flower-framed garden;
Counts the mysteries by moments,
In earth tones, and rhythm and blues,
As moss-covered memories from cocktails and conversation,
At dusk on the porch of the Columns Hotel.

Molly Quinn, March 31, 2014

Upon reading Mary Aswell Doll's (2017) *The Mythopoetics of Currere:
Memories, Dreams, and Literary Texts as Teaching Avenues to Self-Study*,
I am at first overcome, flooded with powerful feelings, images, stories,
words; and I find myself insufficient before the task of trying to articulate
it significance, to compose of them some sense and sensibility for others to
receive. Never mind trying to do any justice to her immeasurably resonant
and rich reveries and tantalizing and tentacular[1] teachings—fecund fruits,
teeming threads. Perhaps, it is that her work has summoned up that sense
of "moreness" of which Huebner (1995) speaks, her thinking and writing
tapping into the spirit of things—that *more* than we know, can ever know,
that confronts us, at the edge of our limits and end of our knowings, at
once surprising, humbling, disturbing, comforting, which moves us beyond

our present knowns, our present selves even, birthing within us something other, different and new (pp. 15–16)—or uncovering that already within as such, heretofore othered or unbeknown.

While anyone who has sought to venture into the method of *currere*[2] can attest—and I use that word "method" here in its etymological sense as a way, journey, quest, and pursuit beyond behind, between, among, after (*OED*, 1989)—this reflective inquiry and practice engaging the interdisciplinary and autobiographical study of educational experience[3] can profoundly advance our understanding, and contribute to the productive reconstruction of self, society, and subject matter, and their relations too (Pinar, 2012): the courses of study taken, to be sure, as well as the courses of our lives. Yet, Doll (2017) here actually enacts, undergoes, takes us beneath too, this illuminating art, this transformational study of experience, in the writing and presentation of it. We might say she embodies, conjures, incarnates, it: performs the spirit, and soul[4] of *currere* in her work. And, in such, she makes it possible for us to enter into, to perceive and feel, to be moved and changed by what she sets forth as well. The fruits tasted, the threads gathered, simultaneously thus also take us to our own experience—memories and dreams, texts and teachings in and of our own lives—and to new fruitful, thread-woven makings (i.e., poetics/*poesis*)[5] of our own therein and thereof. Of some mythic proportions indeed, as well, related as they are to spirit and soul, touching something perhaps ancient, archetypal, *daimonic*,[6] divine, supernatural, or preternatural: a sense of something significant, animating, illuminating, and even sacred, if not fictional too.

I suddenly remember then "New Orleans at Dusk" and this poem[7] I scrawled there once upon a time, having had recently returned home from New York City where I then lived. To be sure New Orleans, spirit and soul prolific, is a place of much literary character, Catholic and carnivalesque: teeming with dark fictions, mythic depths, romantic texts, and shadowy dreams—a legendary and haunted city, having borne tortuous roads of tormented ancestry, and great burdens of history grand and grotesque; home of saints, sinners, vampires, voodoo queens, angels, demons, ghosts and specters of innumerable stripes. Summoning memory, *currere*, too, does oft take our thoughts toward home, but I think it is more that I first met Mary in New Orleans, or so I imagine it. She then lived there in a nearby suburb, and I, as a graduate student at LSU, began enjoying with her the, oh so many, parties (garden and not) and dinners—at the time, in the French Quarter—of Bill Pinar, "hosting . . . to listen, gesturing and pouring wine" of which she also speaks (Doll, 2017, p. 9), and of others, as well as a host of lively "curricularist" events besides: intellectual revelries, delicious spirited gatherings embracing body and soul as well as mind in a kind of kindred community. *Embodied creole care courting not the unending march of progress . . .* perhaps.

Then, it also may be NOLA[8] itself, in noting these two decisive ideas from Jung's (1963) autobiography—that resonate strongly with her also—ghosts, and synchronicity (p. xi-xii)—and the curricular considerations such posed too. *The phoenix rising up, perpetual return,* and rebirth. *The soft sustaining sciences of sensuality, underbelly understandings, rooted revelations. The tucked-away, hidden treasures and pleasures, momentary mysteries, moss-covered memories, and cocktail conversations* . . . connecting. All also *in earth tones, and rhythm and blues.* Doll's work unveils, even revels in, such Gaia goddess knowledges, underworld wisdom wanderings ensuing Eros, in contrast to the linear, logical, full light of consciousness lauded by/in conventional curriculum, which in seeking to standardize minds instigates, rather, death of the human spirit (Pinar, 1994, p. 197; Doll, 2017, p. 128). She gathers:

> We are less ego and more psyche.[9] The Great Work we should be doing is mining our own inner resources for their teachings about our foibles, fears, and fantasies. This is the Great Work of *currere.*
>
> (Doll, 2017, p. 39)

It is the unconscious—and its reality which is poetic, not scientific (p. 39)—that Doll would have us, then, educationally more attend: this "hidden, creative power that sustains culture and selfhood alike" (p. 39), as she asserts too that "true knowledge is really wisdom which comes from unseen places" (p. 58). In this, also, she brings attention via *currere*: not only to the curriculum as the course of study—the term etymologically drawn from a course for running, in concert with the course of life run, and the infinitive "to run" addressing the lived experience thereof (Pinar & Grumet, 1976/2014)—but also to this "inner coursing" itself, the current running, flowing, from within (Doll, 2017, p. 128), the power and "pull of the inner life" (p. xi), that makes meaning, movement, metamorphosis, possible—albeit, as the lotus flower, most oft found shrouded and apt to bloom amid mud and murky waters too.

Herein, we can be said to access hidden dimensions of the self, that ghost the self, and "ghosts of history" in our midst as well (p. xii). *Earth tones*, in synchronic *rhythm and blues.* Actually, "brown study" (Ransome, 1962) Doll likens to the work of *currere*, like that so-called describing melancholy,[10] as it summons the inward turn, and deep contemplation. She notes here, as well, via Turco (2004, p. 162), that such fosters the awakening of the imagination too, the province of poetics, and as the road to revelation, the way to wisdom. Jung, Doll explains, calls the step into the murkiness of this other ghostly reality an 'act of grace'" (Jung, 1963, p. 199, as cited in in Doll, 2017, p. xii).[11]

And thus, Mary[12] brings this grace, or act thereof, to curriculum, to *currere*, for us, by embracing its *mythopoetics*, enticing us to its embrace too. As engaging ways imaginative and metaphorical, she notes the relation of *mythopoetics* to literature—a subject too she has taught for over half a century—and endorses fiction in this way as making possible "an opening to self-knowing," "a doorway to the self," which "helps us uncover our own fictions that exile us" (p. xv). She endorses the teaching of literature too to "connect students . . . to what courses within them. Mythic stories . . . dark, providing the opportunity to explore the unknown" (p. xv). Via the *mythopoetics* of *currere*, she elaborates, we unearth that which is hidden, in the shadows, the fictions we live—the images and metaphors, the psychic life beneath, without which we are without soul, the *mythopoetics* of *currere* "setting the imagination free" (p. xvi).

One hears echoes here of Maxine Greene (1995)—of archetypal significance, if there were such a thing, in the kingdom of education—who also educationally endeavored over and emphasized the import of "releasing the imagination," and the powerful role of literature and all the arts therein. And she, too, spoke of work. The great work for us, as she described it, is to "lend our life to the work" of art, and by such, to labor to "achieve" it (Greene, 1980/2001, p. 12). For, such works "offer each of us visions *for us*—if we are willing to open ourselves to them, to attend" (p. 12). For Doll (2017), via *currere*, they engage us in achieving ourselves and our own lives as works of art, mythically, mythopoetically, in the making as well—and subversively, transformatively, so. I disrupt tradition myself here by citing Doll at some length concerning such:

> The "mythopoetics" of *currere* offers such transformations by way of literature, where "worlds open through imaginative alterity" (Pinar, 2011, p. 100). Worlds-without can become worlds-within. (p. 139)
>
> We enter a world that surprises us so much, that we begin to see the delights that unfold from the other side of things. (p. 73)
>
> Seeing archetypally is educationally significant . . . provides a new dispensation for teaching and learning . . . designed from the inside out, turning current curriculum practice around.
>
> (p. 43)

Soft sciences of sensuality. Underbelly understandings. Rooted revelations. In calling us to the inside-out and other-sidedness of things, Doll (2017) flips the script—post-scripts, pre-scripts, de-scripts, counter-scripts—regarding conventional curriculum and orthodox education, upending its prevailing literalism,[13] overturning its anesthetizing, prosaic effect; and she affirms the "ever-changing" "livingness of life" and our efforts to understand it (p. 49):

words, works, worlds—alive, and living. She, of course, achieves such, as we have gleaned, via *currere*, and its mythopoetic address; yet I want to explore the significance of such here a bit further, if only briefly, particularly as salient for our present curriculum labors and perhaps those to come, principally through her engagement with fiction therein—specifically her attention to key characteristics thereof "that allow students and teachers to live in language differently, more poetically, less literally," and that create a "place for the work that *currere* encourages" (p. 50). These features of fiction simultaneously ask us to engage experience anew respecting such: familiarity/foreignness, slowness/speed, and fluidity/fixedness as well as that which I will touch on only in concluding this, my serenade to the mythopoetics of *currere*, as so integrally akin to address of the others—food/famine.

Foraging and Facing Familiar and Foreign Via the Mythopoetics of *Currere*

> A world will overcome you, the happiness, the abundance, the incomprehensible beauty of a world. Live a while in the books, learn from them.
>
> —(Rilke, 1934/1993, p. 25)

In the worlds fiction brings (to) us, brings us into, we encounter both that which is familiar and that which is unfamiliar, Doll (2017) notes, even radically so, concerning character, time, place, plot, and language, and this oft simultaneously, synchronistically so. The commonplace succumbs to strange enchantment and inexplicability—the familiar de-familiarized; we find ourselves somehow too in intimate and compelling relation with/to that which is at once also utterly other and foreign, far removed existentially from our own lives and experiences, yet speaking to/of us still. Doll reminds us of fiction's capacity here to "de-literalize deadened imaginations" (p. 50)—echoes of her ghost awakenings and visitations, and synchronicities, in our midst, perhaps as well. If we enter in, and attend, words are themselves revivified, in a sense; as Doll explains, via Hillman (1975, p. 9), we discern traces of the writer's mind and style, and come to experience "that words contain angels; they are emissaries with etymologies" (Doll, 2017, p. 50). Her focus is on fiction's difference (presenting the foreign and/or making the familiar so)—what Gadamer (1975/2013) calls "the text's alterity" (p. 282)—and the destabilization engagement with it might bring, disrupting routinization, defying dogma. It offers the opportunity—as she so aptly articulates via Biddy Martin (1997)—to encounter "the selvedges of language" (p. 9), referencing "self" and "edge," and the emotional risks and rewards felt therein.

For me, what is called to mind here is Heidegger's (1971) notion of language itself as the house of being, and insinuations regarding the making of the self, and of subjectivity, via discourses and discursive structures—the workings of language (Foucault, 1969/1972) at the heart also of the disciplines we teach and the stories into which we are spun at birth, our becoming in narratives in *medias res*, as it were, and already in the making: bio-graphies. Curricularly, such workings of language alert us anew to the power and import of history, and memory (Pinar, 2011), threads reaching before and beyond us and in which we are entangled, as well as our forgetfulness therein, our propensity to thoughtlessly accept the given, "coerced by cultural demands" (Doll, 2017, p. 47). Engaging such might too "reveal the extent to which history can be re-membered and re-conceptualized when the ghosts of the past or of the psyche are resurrected" (p. xii) via the heightened experience[14] of familiar and foreign that fiction affords, and which our curriculum writ large, from manifold "chimney corner(s)" (p. 47),[15] especially via *currere*, might also compel.

Otherness—evoking the foreign, that which we educationally bring to students—is a name Huebner (1995) gives curriculum itself—not only teaching described as being with others in language, but also calling students to participate with/in the otherness of each other, the world, the teacher, the self, in the hope that such encounters don't ultimately overwhelm or overthrow but rather open and advance understanding: a ground to stand upon, support in the midst of sustained challenge and enriched transformation—an eye ever to our "not yet" and "to come," ever-present incompletion and thus possibility, "the lure of the transcendent," expanding horizons, as well. Such is a matter of attending and awakening to the journey of self, with others, of life, riddled with the familiar and foreign with which to reckon (Wang, 2004). In this way, we might remember that curriculum itself need find its work herein, as well; many of our ancestors say as much concerning a necessary call in/of education to/for: the mind's liberation/illumination (Kliebard, 2004), *conscientization* (Freire, 1970/1995), wide-awakeness (Greene, 1988), response-ability in relation to the renewal of the world (Arendt, 1954/1993). In contemporary parlance, we must be "woke" (Guillory, 2019).[16] Reflectively facing time and again that which is foreign, and its face in the familiar, is requisite to such. As music- and mythmakers and dreamers-of-dreams,[17] we must ever seek ways to arouse anew, re-rouse, ourselves and others, re-membering and re-conceiving/conceptualizing ourselves and our relations via meetings with otherness from without and within.

Certainly *currere* supports such; entering into its mythopoetics furthers this movement—the story(ies) of others, other(ed) stories, as story-starters, ignited sparks rebirthing consciousness (Chu, 2019) from deep, mythic, terrestrial grounds—our inner coursings, the courses of our lives, our curricular conversations, too. Doll's (2017) refreshing exhale[18] in expounding here beckons us through the unfolding of our own otherness, expressing an "intention to invite engagement with the strange inner workings of our lives, glimpsed as through a glass darkly when reading others' lives" (p. 116).[19] Such an engagement is an "opening out in a situation of estrangement that affirms life's possibilities" (p. 101) and enables us "to see what knowledge is hiding" (p. 101). In reconnecting to that which courses within us, we recover what she refers to as our own curricular material, including our mythic kin "from the deeper past who haunt us" (p. 28); *grotesque* and *grotto-esque* (Salvio, 2007, p. 50; Doll, 2017, p. 117), we "open our portals to what lies beyond, beside, or below the surface" (p. 66). In attending to these deep-down matters, loosening our reliance upon reason alone, Doll contends that with memory and myth[20] we can think anew, and access wisdom for the sojourn ahead, which also inspires new ways of being and becoming concerning curriculum and pedagogy, and our theories and practices as teachers and scholars (p. 48). At this time, too, such efforts are all the more important, and critical, in order to counter an on-the-clock, contemporary, conformist context of decontextualized accountability commanding linear, literalist learning and standardized, scripted curriculum—at some unprecedented pace too.[21] In redressing such, Doll evokes in us the question: how might we more fully take up the mythopoetic, *currere*, the mythopoetics of *currere*, and the illuminating ruminations upon the familiar and foreign herein, in all of our curriculum musings and makings, wonderings and worldings?[22]

In Praise of Slow: Of Curriculum, Poetics, and the Mythic Time of Texts

> Back home in Louisiana. . . . Ordinary life there, it also affirmed this way: hot, humid, heavy aromatic air—the plenty and thick of it; and wet, fragrant, fertile soil, soul-sinking and -settling swampland, swallowing and swaddling clothes; flora and fauna as fecund and fragrant and furrowing, grand old live oaks with upraised and outstretched brooding branches and strong, broad- and deep-reaching roots, nests and cradles, cypress "knees"—knots tying threads to everywhere.[23] Time slowed to a hot pot of simmering coffee brewing on the stovetop.
>
> (Quinn, 2011, p. 1215)

An additional portrait of home comes to mind: *the everydayness of life . . . in the languid, slow, easy city.* Yet, even—perhaps especially—the ordinary is not without archetypal dimensions to unearth, or mythic depths to follow;

albeit, here, the point being that it's all a matter of time. Years before "New Orleans at Dusk," I penned the above as I began contemplating lived experience at the nexus of globalization, citizenship, and education: what Hansen (2008) describes as an overwhelming feeling in contemporary times of accelerating acceleration (p. 289). It's a time against time, curriculum a race against it too somehow. Jardine (2014) articulates it well:

> But here is a school reality that is hard to admit: those sorts of work that fit the clock-work, one-thing-after-another, always accelerating rush of empty time bully themselves to the front of the line and provide a way to not just marginalize but humiliate those who might suggest that there is thoughtfulness, rigorousness, authenticity and good work to be had out from under this running-out panic.
>
> (p. 68)

Curriculum, the course of time running-out. He goes on to locate school bullying at the very heart of the institution, as constituted through the lens of efficiency, wherein the work of "intellectual whiling"—engaging that which is memorable, rich in relatedness, commanding sustained attention and rewarding such—is disavowed, deemed all too weighty and wasteful. "Little in school tasks organized thus . . . is worth *while*"[24] (Jardine, 2014, p. 69).

However, to genuinely attend—to the inner life, the matter beneath, the mythos within, the worth *while*; to take up that which Doll (2017) advocates, takes time. Considering fiction in relation to such, we settle down and nestle in with a good book; we attune ourselves to its rhythm as we enjoy drinking in and savoring its storied sweetness. We might say that the poetic is born and experienced via this art of attending, which is also a matter of slowing down. Doll (2017) invites us to tarry and dawdle, and asks us via slowness, highlighting this quality of fiction, to address such, too, in the teaching of it, and in *currere* engagement through it:

> Reading aloud . . . attending to punctuation . . . where all the varieties of instants grow. Giving students time to linger over passages, to dwell inside them, is a gift teachers can afford to offer. Slowing the pace . . . to allow for silence.
>
> (pp. 50–51)

Sumara (1996) speaks similarly of the magic performed in a teacher's reading to students from a novel, summoning new possibilities into existence, and shared experiences that resonate. Vaquer (2016) draws explicit lines between curriculum and poetics, and explores poetry's possibilities herein, the teaching of it, highlighting also the aural/oral elements therein—its musicality, noting too Morris' (2009) assertion that "music gets expressed through unformulated experience" (p. 11). We might say that Doll (2017) invites us as well as her students to entertain and articulate such unformulated experience, engaging its mythopoetics via *currere*, as such resonates with us in reading fiction. *Rhythm and blues. Languid, slow, easy* . . . long listening and lingering.

In devoting a chapter of her text to this important art of idleness—lingering, loafing, dwelling—Vaquer (2016) also acknowledges that work undertaken in schools rarely encourages aesthetic experience requiring such: poetry itself is subject to rubricification, and the study of literature to instrumentalization. In contrast, she affirms poetry and educational explorations of it via the lens of Dewey's (1934) *Art as Experience*—and traditions in curriculum studies that also embrace as much—wherein by such slow whiling, one enjoys delicious connection, interaction, with a work; wherein one experiences "heightened vitality"—"experience in the degree in which it *is* experience," as Dewey would say (1934, p. 19)—as one comes out of oneself, becomes one with the work, and world, finding oneself anew therein too. Such, alas however, seems at odds with society's (and its education system's) (over)emphasis on efficiency (and its cousin, economic productivity), in concert with pervasive legacies related to positivism, scientism, capitalism, literalism, neoliberalism, and the Protestant work ethic, to name a few (e.g., Taubman, 2009; Pinar, 2012; Doll 1994; Jardine, 2014).

As early as 1934, Dewey noticed a growing presence of the "hurried and impatient" (p. 46) in our midst, interfering with experience itself, speedily undertaken without realized perception, reflection, or meaning—via what he describes as a zeal for/excess of doing, a "lust for action," as well as at the other extreme, a surplus of receptivity (p. 46). Such intemperance, it seems, is something to which education is particularly susceptible, akin to what Wiggins and McTighe (2005) denote as the "twin sins" of curriculum design, committed by focusing all too easily and simply either on "activity" or on "coverage"—what students will do or what content will be delivered to them (p. 16). And we forget to take time, to give students time, respecting any of all such, too, in a clock-bound culture bent on speed (Seidel, 2014). Through poetry, then, the leisure of the poetic, perhaps ironically enough, the time of texts, so slow as it were, we may find some redemption of experience.

Such temporality, of course, speaks not simply to poetry, fiction, and its teaching, nor even pedagogy, curriculum, and education, but rather to a cultural ethos writ large. To consider slowness in this way is akin to embracing the art, the mythopoetics, the aesthetic experience, of living, we might say. The Slow Movement,[25] an international effort of global reach, officially launched via its first manifesto and meeting of delegates from 15 countries in 1989, "has gained recognition as a way to resist both globalization and the frantic pace of contemporary life" (Berg & Seeber, 2013, p. 7) in advocating *slow*—wherein life, living, making a living, may be savored and substantive, not simply efficient or expedient—and involving attention to apt pace, returned from advanced speed, to quality from quantity.

Its origins in the Slow Food Movement, incited by Carlo Petrini's protest of the opening of a McDonald's in Rome in 1986, illuminate something further concerning the heart of its address. In contesting fast food, this organization has sought to preserve traditional, regional cuisine and cooking, and the practices that sustain such, respecting local farming practices and ecosystems. Such contest includes what we might call a resistance to fast food living,[26] by which, without care, we are compelled to hurriedly feed on/consume that which rather than nourishing us actually diminishes our health and well-being (and that of others, and of the planet too). The focus herein, then, is on that which sustains and renews more broadly, given only in genuinely recovering the slowness of human relation and reflection, of being more fully present together in the world. Evidence of this kind of cultural critique and action in the direction of "slow" can be seen at least, for example, in the rise of interest among many in such things as meditation, yoga practice, and Buddhism, as well as organic food and farm-to-table dining.

While the slow concept has taken root in some of these daily lived ways, and in a number of other arenas of human endeavor (e.g., the organization Cittaslow—"slow cities," slow architecture, slow business)—albeit difficult to say with what ultimate success, given the globalized strength of and our collective attachment to speed/"fast" as well as inequitable disparities impacting experience thereof—it has yet to be fully taken up in curriculum studies.[27] Curriculum scholars have, nonetheless, addressed similar concerns, and there are efforts to articulate "slow education" (Barker, 2012) as a response to the pressures ensuing from the proliferation of standardized curricula, teaching, and high-stakes testing, which might advance more personal, culturally sustaining, and qualitatively evaluative approaches in education. Berg and Seeber (2013), in an article prelude to their book endorsing the "slow professor" (2016), seek to apply the idea to the work of the academy, aptly articulating what is on offer and what is at stake herein:

> It is, as Parkins and Craig put it, "a process whereby everyday life— in all its pace and complexity, frisson and routine—is approached with care and attention . . . an attempt to live in the present in a meaningful, sustainable, thoughtful and pleasurable way" (2006, p. ix). . . . the Slow movement has the "potential" to not only "reinvigorate . . . everyday life" (2006, p. 119) but also "repoliticize . . . everyday life" (2006, p. 135).

As Jennifer Lindholm and Katalin Szelényi conclude, "it is critical that we . . . strive to develop habits of conducting our work and our lives in ways that promote both our own and others' well-being" (2008, p. 36). Corporatisation not only speeds up the clock but also compromises academic values. By taking the time for deliberation, reflection, and dialogue, the Slow Professor takes back the intellectual life of the university.

(Berg & Seeber, 2013, p. 6)

This work, no doubt, may afford further generative insight into the significance of the concept of slowness. It may stimulate the promising pursuit of it in curriculum studies—where deep thinking, thoughtful reflection, sustained study, and thorough inquiry is no luxury (p. 5), but rather a necessity, and certainly of serious import. Good work is not unrelated to good food, good stories, and . . . good time(s).

Doll (2017), in hearkening to the slowness of fiction in her work, opens us up in her way to the abundance of slowness. Jardine (2014) might add that good stories also offer the virtues of slowness, not only in enticing us to gather, tarry, and return, but also in teaching us this by actually necessitating it, obliging such—we learn to while therein (p. 87)—a kind of magic, wonder, gift, unto itself. Doll (2017) might point further to the *great* stories as work, woven and whiled away, where we bring our inner lives, our memories and myths, the coursings within—where we meet, linger, and revisit via *currere*, inspiring resurrection and rebirth too. Sumara (1996) also agrees. Drawing on Heidegger's (1971) notion of *dwelling*, involving care and attention in living and abiding in a place with others, Sumara (1996) explains that "literary fiction asks for [such] dwelling, for it is only by dedicating oneself to the difficulty and ambiguity of dwelling with the text that a commonplace for interpretation and understanding can be evoked" (p. 181). Alluding as such to that sense of otherness, complexity, difference, and depth, he summons us back to Doll's (2017) attunement to the mythic.

And so while there is this attention to time,[28] time not wholly unaddressed in the field of curriculum, as something of a persistent problem therein, increasingly so given present historical (political, social, cultural, global, etc.) forces—and even glimmers of these turns toward deceleration and slowness, so to speak; there might, and perhaps ought to be, much more so. Doll (2017) makes this needed address intentional and explicit not only forwarding the "slowness" of fiction and its teaching, but also taking time to the mythic dimension: otherworldly, out of time, out of step with *chronos* time—which is quantitative, chronological, sequential, linear. Via *currere*, too, in relating a back-to-school dream of hers, wherein was featured a broken clock, she describes being called to "delve into a vaster time of myths and ancient knowings," which is also a call from the unconscious to wider and deeper understanding (p. 35).

We tap into the eternity of the present, cyclical time, wherein subject and object are one, subjectivity and subject matter no longer severed (Doll, 2017, p. 62). We learn from time: fleeting and fragile, old and deep, ecological and relational, contingent and creative, earthy and grounded (Seidel, 2014, pp. 182–183), nurturing intimacy with knowledge and with life, contemplatively "as a way of gathering insight and stillness together" (p. 177).

Perhaps I have spent here too much time on time, slowing too much into slow, yet via this mythic face of time too we are bidden to more rightfully consider—as this dream of Doll's (2017) continues to illuminate for her via two stones that all of a sudden break through a small opening in a window and land just beside her: "the earth and its elements are organic, alive, and have with intention" (p. 35), carrying and speaking in a time of their own, that we are perhaps meant to attend.

Curriculum Coursings and Currents of Life: From Fixedness to Fluidity and Flow

> *And then I thought, let me follow this and see where it leads. . . . I was arrested by a picturesque view—a stony dirt path leading down to the water, hovered over by an old brick bridge, grasses anointing and stony brook music filling my ears, framed too by lovely wildflowers—purples, yellows, bright reds, verdant green—and sweet dragonflies, bees and butterflies, orange and yellow, flitting about from flower to flower, rejoicing in and contributing to such beauty. . . . And so I enjoyed this uplifting moment there and by the water's edge. Others, having found their nooks, sat with me, embracing and abiding therein too. I, of course, found a large stone rock, from which to perch myself from view for a bit . . . listening to the rushing water, looking at the intricacy with which the tree roots before me wrapped themselves around, and entwined with, the myriad stones—uprooted and yet nourished. The stones too, all broken, pieces large and small, as if by artistic design arranged about, upon, beneath and atop each other. . . . All dancing and conversing together—roots and rocks, as the waters kissed them all, reaching in to join the party. . . . I think I wanted here to pen all to remember.*
>
> —*(Molly Quinn, Spring 2015)*

Nature often speaks to me. I could not include this journal entry in its entirety for its length but if I had, the reader would hear the many voices of my elders and ancestors herein too: the gentle soothing of my dear mother, a gardener and lover of gardens, who had just recently passed, summoned by the sight of pink Mimosa pom-poms, prevalent in the play of my childhood; Michelangelo on the sculptural work of art hidden already within the stone; the "Two Bills," as they were oft affectionately called at LSU, Bill Doll and Bill Pinar, brought to mind by the butterflies who accompanied me on my stroll—their beautiful "butterfly effects"[29] in my life considered anew, the most recent at the time an invitation by Bill Pinar to edit a collection on Bill Doll's contributions to curriculum studies: *just with the one thought, invitation, email, was ushered a return to connection with so many beloved, and if not yet even known very well, kindred others, into a conspiracy of love via this work. And I get to be a part of it . . .* (Quinn, 2015). And here, I note nothing of all the mythic and psychic stirrings present as well, respecting butterflies, trees, stones—circles of stones, Stonehenge, turning to stone, the stones would cry out, etc.

Doll (2017), challenging and critiquing the fixedness with which curriculum, education, seems typically so endeared, points then to this quality of fluidity via fiction, and as remedy to such, what we might embrace when "our [reifications and] repressions sit like stones" (p. 4), thought sedimented, literally binding. Contemplating time, too, as liquid, she illumines how, via the mythopoetics of *currere*, we might rather enter into the wellspring of life's complexity, interconnectedness, relationality—*witnessing, testifying, well-placed welcoming, mysteries by moments, ancient lore, connecting and commanding attention.* Such reminds of Lather's (2007) incitement via our scholarly inquiry to "work the ruins" in our midst. Doll (2017) speaks—from stone—of our need to study the runes "in the company of others to complicate our thinking about self and world" (p. 4). Ruminating on ruins, on runes. Opening to the flexible indefinite, the mutable uncertainty, exemplified and encountered via fiction, and the multiple temporalities—synchronicities—and mythical manifestations ensuing, especially as accompanied by autobiographical entanglements and undertakings via *currere*, we come to know anew "the natural world as pulsating and alive. There is more than one's consciousness . . . it is all around us" (p. 67).

Furthering such, we might take it up in our manner of teaching, Doll suggests, as well: She describes the making of a place for developing such relatedness, neither teacher nor text as sole author, performance, improvisation at work, where many voices and sounds come together, mingling, actively engaged in making "living bonds" that define relationships rather than create separating walls (p. 51). One formally thinks concerning curriculum: verticality, horizontality, spiral, inter/cross/multi/trans-disciplinarity. "Seeping" is the simply delicious word Doll uses, which stories when shared have a way of doing (p. 51)—*knots tying threads to everywhere.*

> To navigate the difficult passages of one's journey in life, one needs a thread. It is the thread that connects one not only to the exit but to the entrance, to one's beginnings . . . to the archetypes found in myth . . . to those mistresses of destiny, the Fates. (p. xii-xiii)

As Virginia Woolf (1929/1957) put it, "Fiction is like a spider's web, attached ever so lightly perhaps, but still attached to life at all four corners" (p. 43). The webbed connections fiction weaves go to the root of one's being.

(pp. 47–48)

Roots and rocks . . . and the spinning of spiders. Perhaps it is unsurprising that Ashanti folklore features Ananse, the spider, and in one tale tells of how he brought the gift of story to the world. For once, there were no stories to be told or heard upon earth; all were kept in a golden box, sealed, and in the possession of Nyame, the sky god. Having spun a web to the heavens, Ananse petitioned to purchase this treasure, and as the trickster, he was able to meet the sky god's impossible price. He took the golden box back to his village, and upon opening it, all the stories scattered throughout the world, with us still. Stories, from heaven like manna, bread, *attached to life at all four corners*. I am reminded of a description here, too, on the art of interpreting texts, a process wherein, heretofore hidden from us by distraction, "the world . . . flutters open and its interdependencies become more and more experienceable" (Jardine, 2014, p. 154). Jardine here continues, likening such to Gadamer's discussion of *Bildung*—"becoming experienced," a German idea upon which much of education there and elsewhere has been grounded: leading to "an *increasing* susceptibility and vulnerability in one's ability to experience of the fabrics and textures of the world . . . more and more *lovable* . . ." (p. 154).

Much more is ever afoot than the mind we are most apt to attend—in education and via curriculum—admits: ancestral, earthy, ecological, and other. Doll (2017) speaks of current events as also events with currents (p. 7). Fiction, as fluid—and in its mythic modes, wherein our own *currere* coursings enter into the thick with this flow—recalls for us "the sense that trees breathe, the cosmos speaks, things change shape" and "show[s] us the aliveness of life, including death" (p. 66), "the mystery of death intertwined with life" (p. 71). Relatedly, among the most recent of times that I've actually seen Mary Doll, I will never forget: Victoria, British Columbia, January 2018. I had arrived early to the wake of my beloved mentor who had recently passed, Bill Doll, her former husband. At the funeral home, I was at first told that I must wait, that it was the family's time for visitation with the body. Yet, a few moments later, the attendant returned, ushering me in, sharing something that was most moving to me: "Mary and her son Will said you are family." Embracing the relationality Doll (2017) endorses in her work makes of us all kin, sustenance for each other, in life and in death.

Serenade to the Soul of *Currere*: A Veritable Feast for Curriculum Studies

I began this serenade to Mary Aswell Doll and her *Mythopoetics of Currere* (2017) most sweet, with a fiesta, festival, fete, of my own poetic post-Mardi Gras musings, birthed in New Orleans, brought to mind by her work, as the place of our first meeting, and more. The words, too, had poured from me while feasting—NOLA also a renowned abode for such—on Creole cuisine at the Columns Hotel; but I was feasting on much more than that: on moments and mysteries and memories too. I savored much, as well, the "good" words like wine, the simmering and satiating stories, served also therein—bubbling over bitter and sweet as ghosts and grand oaks gathered too, toasting to ancient insight and wellspring wisdom as well as new hope and the promise of possibility, even amid darkness, doubt and difficulty too. Such was cooked up, as well, in the writing by autobiographical reflection— engaging experientially anew what Doll calls us to: entertaining familiar and foreign, in slowing down, as we return to, enter into, the, oh-so-fluid currents within and world-connected too. Drawing in these ways to that which fiction, by its character, can teach us, and in her work writ large, she not only demonstrates quenchingly so this culinary art, its mythopoetics, via *currere*, but prepares for us through such as well a table of inspired tastings, fulfilling and fruitful: "soul" food, food for the soul, in the making—mythic depths, embodied understandings, fruit of the earth shining through; goddesses and gods, and monsters and mortals, and their stories too, all in attendance.

Additionally, as indeed offering food, sustenance, that for which the soul hungers, that which satisfies the soul—this is how Doll (2017) depicts fiction too, likening such also to that which many curriculum theorists seek to educationally advocate, particularly via *currere*. Inhabiting its spirit, she shows and incites us to feel what Huebner (1995) suggests is our work: attending to the journey of the soul. We yearn, as she explains, for story and memory, structurally rooted, grounded "in the depths of our consciousness" (Doll, 2017, p. 52)—meeting and making for knowledge within, a kind of intimacy of which we are starved by literalism. Our stories, our ways with words, as bread, we hear them, we tell them, and are fed, and feed others with them as well—earth-world myths, unconscious collectivities, echoing through them too; and offering us "nothing less than a sense of life itself" (Wright, 1937/1966, p. 24). Indeed, Mary, in this work, graces, brings this grace to, blesses us by saying grace before this feast for curriculum studies. "Perhaps our hunger will help us find our own words to express our own selves and our stories" (Doll, 2017, p. 52), she prays. "Think of it. Our symposia could become a banquet, a matter of caring for the soul" (p. 52). I pray we'll continue to chew on that, with cocktails, over our moss-covered memories and curriculum conversations too.

Notes

1. I draw this word from Haraway (2016), who in the context of an earth ecosystem in crisis turns to what she calls the "Chthonic powers of Terra"—the tentacular feelers, many, deeply rooted, and travelling in manifold directions, as of a spider—that are needed to tell our stories, to make of ourselves multispecies kin, to "stay with the trouble" and become capable of response together in the midst of our inescapable and entangled relationality. Doll's (2017) work affirms as well the chthonic—the wisdom of snakes and spiders, for instance, and the underworld understandings to be gleaned in entering into the depths of the earth and its stories, in which we are enmeshed.

2. For more on the *currere* method, see Pinar and Grumet (1976/2014) and Pinar (2012). The reader will find further discussion thereof in the present text that illumines something of its origins and meanings, albeit specifically as focused on Doll's (2017) engagement thereof.

3. This method is systematic, outlined in four phases addressing regressive, progressive, analytical, and synthetical aspects of inquiry, enabling in this way what Dewey (1938/1997) described is the work of education itself, the reconstruction of experience (p. 47). We might say it is described well by what William Doll (1994) advocated via his 4R's, that curriculum be recursive, rich, rigorous, and relational.

4. Kovel (1991) describes soul as the spiritual form taken by the self.

5. Trueit (2005) takes up the power of the poetic, *poesis*—to make, to create, to compose (OED, 1989)—in/as creating, yet also in/as re-presenting: to re-tell a story, for instance, engages elements ancient and new, the power thereof in the experience—embodied, aesthetic, spirit summoned and felt therein (Trueit, 2005). Akin, we have "*aesthesis*, which means at root a breathing in . . . of the world, the gasp, 'aha,' the 'uh' of the breath of wonder . . . and aesthetic response" (Hillman, 2006, p. 36).

6. Doll (2017), in her work, takes up this notion of the *daimonic*, that within each of us that bears our destiny but which we have forgotten. She suggests too that the regressive move of *currere* supports us in the necessary work of recovering this energy or image that directs and yet haunts our lives, which also allows us to see our actions in relation to this energy or image—and the pattern belonging and essential to it. She grounds such an idea in the work of Hillman (1996) via Plato who posited the existence of such a *daimon*, that a particular image informs every life in this way, the acorn of the unknown self, integrally tied to much of our personal potential, purpose, and path. Myss (2002) speaks of it in terms of a sacred contract, of getting in touch with our archetypes in order to awaken the divine power within. She describes too her own resistance for many years to the work to which she was called, wherein lied the gifts she had been given in this life.

7. A poem seemed an apt way to begin this work. The reader is apt to find also more pepperings of the poetic throughout this text than is anticipated in scholarly writing. Additional excesses too are to be found, and as meant to imbue as possible Doll's (2017) work, the mythopoetics of *currere*, within my own here, and embody something of its attendings: my own autobiographical interweaving, and extensive footnoting. I trust these indulgences also call attention to her ruminations/illuminations upon the relationality, interconnectivity, and synchronicity, as well as the ghosts, threads, hidden and layered depths and

breadths, more-than-meets-the eyes of mystery and meaning that make up our lives—and literature, curriculum and teaching in relation to such.

8. Acronym for New Orleans, LA.

9. The work of Bernie Neville (1989/2014), who also explores such in *Educating Psyche: Imagination, Emotion and the Unconscious in Learning*, may be of interest to the reader. Quinn (2007a, 2007b) examines, as well, the ways in which psyche has been stripped of soul via the history of psychology, the field's dominance in education, and the imitative frameworks of both disciplines in relation to hard or quantitative science.

10. Doll (2017) notes here scholarship in curriculum studies engaging histories that haunt, like that of Pinar (2006) respecting race and religion in America, and Morris (2001) in relation to memory and the Holocaust.

11. In a chapter on grace and death, between presence and absence, I begin with the vision of my friend, one of the book editors, Mark Bussey: "He imagines grace, and a phenomenology of grace, as 'saving' perhaps indeed herein, wherein reclaimed body wisdom and soul wonder, formerly denied, meet with mind and intellect in resisting the detracted and foreclosed, and in renewing our relation to the earth, to our embodied existence, to each other and beyond" (Quinn, 2020, p. 101). For more respecting grace, see the collection: Bussey and Mozzini-Alister (2020).

12. I am playing a bit with her name here and its mythic or Catholic incantations: *Hail Mary, Full of Grace, the Lord is with thee.* "What is in a name? Apparently, everything" (Doll, 2017, p. 15). Doll (2017) also writes about her name, and her fabled relationship with her mother, after whom she bears it—respecting self-discovery, twin ancestry, death, and rebirth. There is much of interest in the name Mary one might explore, its etymological ties to bitterness, sorrow and rebellion; beauty, perfection, grace, charm, joy, and love; strength and rule as mistress (of the sea)—protectress of the watery depths of emotion here. The name calls to mind, as well, the dark exploits, tragedy and romance of the Queens of England and Scotland, the magic and mirth of Mary Poppins, the inventive foreshadowings in Frankenstein of Mary Shelley, the demons-delivered Mary Magdalene first to testify to the resurrection, and of course, the Virgin Mary with whom I began, Queen of Heaven, Divine Feminine, goddess in many different faces and forms, with links also to Athena who was known for the art of war and of weaving (Ravynstar, 2012; Knight, 2020; Online Etymology Dictionary, n.d.). As synchronicities, strange coincidences, perhaps, would have it, I, too, share "Mary" with Doll—my legally given birth name, about which I also wrote once upon a time in relation to curriculum and hospitality in welcoming the unexpected Other visited upon one, and also from within (Quinn, 2009).

13. Doll (2017) describes it this way: "The opposite of imagination is literalism . . . the problem in our culture is not illiteracy but the literalisms that make us ill" (p. 49).

14. Dewey (1934) speaks of "the refined and intensified forms of experience that are works of art and the everyday events, doings, and sufferings that are universally recognized to constitute experience" (p. 2). In this way, we could say that *currere* is curriculum as a work of art, engaging one personally and aesthetically in such heightened experience of experience and education as its elevated reconstruction herein.

15. Doll (2017) uses this metaphor in relation to the humanities, devalued and dismissed by other, especially science-based, disciplines. Nonetheless, such tangential abodes, like fiction, she points out, disrupt the status quo, re-route feelings, make way for marginalized imaginings to grow (p. 47).

16. Doll (2017) also speaks of the opportunity here to enter into a different mind concerning things. Such is so important with respect to the so many wrongs our givens oft leave unrealized and un-righted. Our experience, our reality, our world is not the experience, reality, world, nor equal to that of others; always ever partial, and potentially perpetuating oppression et al. in the absence of engaging other perspectives.

17. These designations come from a poem of A. W. O'Shaughnessy, cited in Woods (1966, p. 269).

18. I use this term hearkening to spirit, etymologically connected to the breath, which Doll (2017) summons forth so poignantly in her work, and in relation to engagement with stories via fiction. "Thus the great migratory conspiracies of storytelling, the telling from breath to breath (Illich, 1998), each breath, of course, original, irreplaceable, and necessary in breathing life into the while of worthwhile things. 'If the story does not have that breath of life, all the journeying, all the history, all the mystery, is for naught' (Yolen, 1988, p. 10)" (Jardine, 2014, p. 90).

19. While what is actually referenced herein is Salvio's (2007) intention in her work on Ann Sexton and her teaching of "weird abundance," Doll (2017) affirms such intention throughout her work here as well.

20. Echoing her insights here, Deidre Bailey, in Seidel et al. (2014), paraphrasing Jardine, notes: "I am defined by what I can thus remember, what necessarily exclusive and incomplete host of voices haunts my inner life and work and therefore haunts the world that is open in front of me. This composed and cultivated memory constitutes my openness to what comes to meet me from the world" (p. 108). Doll (2017) enacts, performs, her own mythopoetics of *currere*, remembering through myths including those involving Ariadne, Medea, Inanna, Mimir, Odin, Athena, and Persephone, among others.

21. The push of this advanced pace of life continues to pervade even as in recent times Covid-19, an invisible virus, compelled some retreat regarding such, and hopefully some reflective thought upon its ultimate virtues and values, and costs.

22. I locate this term in the work of Heidegger (1927/1962), wherein world becomes a verb in relation to our participation in world-becoming and world-making. The idea, too, has been taken up and reworked via new materialism to embrace ideas involving that which emerges via our affective, expressive, and agentic entanglement with non-human life, and location, the material and semiotic porosities that might make for our capacity to disrupt normative modes of being and temporalities (Haraway, 2016). Pinar (2009) speaks of "the world" this wise in relation to curriculum and cosmopolitanism: "*working from within* to redress the injustice that defines the world . . . Radhakrishnan's (2008, p. 24) question specifies this pedagogical project of cosmopolitanism: 'Does the human become human in the act of letting the world speak through him or her?' This 'worlding' of subjectivity renders into practice the 'Marxian dictum that to know something is to transform it' (2008, p. 25). Such 'worlding' is enacted through the free play of indirect subjectivity, as the heroic individual 'talks

back' to the world that has confounded—made a 'problem' of—one's life and flesh" (p. 146).

23. This phrase was drawn from an inspired line in Mueller's (1996) poem "Curriculum Vitae." In Mueller (1996). *Alive together: New and selected poems*. Reprinted with permissions from Louisiana State University Press.

24. Such brings to mind here a key question from Spencer (1884/2015) that has long occupied the field: What knowledge is of most worth?

25. First coined in the book *In Praise of Slowness* (2004) by Carl Honorè, "the slow movement" involved his articulation of a slow philosophy and what such could mean for all manner of human endeavors, whereby we might foster quality of life and work over quantity, more fully live the moments of life rather than count them, advance pace apt for the nature of the engagements undertaken, speed suited for the work underway.

26. One could make parallels here to Taubman's (2009) critique of education as it has been transformed into *Teaching by Numbers*. Doll (2017, p. 52) relatedly draws upon Moore (1992) in endorsing slowness as well, who says: "Culturally, we have a plastic esophagus suited perhaps to fast food and fast living, but not conducive to soul, which thrives only when life is taken in in a long, slow process of digestion and absorption" (p. 206).

27. Kauper and Jacobs (2019) posit "slow curriculum" as they endorse creative insubordination in teacher education. Of course, other scholarship in the field, like Doll's (2017), works in the spirit of "slow" without explicitly taking up the discourse or being in express alliance with this larger movement, some of which is cited in this text—for example, Dewey (1934), Sumara (1996), Jardine (2014), Seidel (2014), Vaquer (2016) and Chu (2019)—oft intersecting with aesthetics, ecology and Buddhism as well. Additionally, scholarship returning to the significance of "study" in curriculum studies and the work of education and academic endeavor writ large might be said to subscribe to "slow" as well (e.g., Pinar, 2012). In this vein, Doll (2017) discusses study in terms of a "stepping back and stopping" that animates the anima within (p. 129).

28. Temporality, though, is a concept at the heart of *currere* itself (Pinar, 2012), and it has been taken up in the literature to some extent in this way, and by others as well (e.g., Huebner, 1999; Wang, 2010).

29. This concept in chaos theory describes the sensitive (inter)dependency characterizing complex dynamic systems wherein one small change in initial conditions can make for significant changes, large differences, in later outcomes (Scott, 2007). Bill Doll also introduced me to chaos and complexity theories.

References

Arendt, H. (1993). *Between past and future* (D. Lindley, Trans.). Penguin Books. (Original work published 1954)

Barker, I. (2012, November 2). Find the time for slow education. *Times Educational Supplement*. https://www.tes.com/magazine/archive/find-time-slow-education

Berg, M., & Seeber, B. (2013, April). The slow professor: Challenging the culture of speed in the academy. *Transformative Dialogues: Teaching & Learning Journal*, 6(3), 1–7.

Berg, M., & Seeber, B. (2016). *The slow professor: Challenging the culture of speed in the academy*. University of Toronto Press.

Chu, E. (2019). *Exploring curriculum as an experience of consciousness transformation*. Palgrave Macmillan.

Dewey, J. (1934). *Art as experience*. The Penguin Group.

Dewey, J. (1997). *Experience and education*. Simon & Schuster, Inc. (Original work published 1938)

Doll, M. A. (2017). *The mythopoetics of currere: Memories, dreams, and literary texts as teaching avenues to self-study*. Routledge.

Doll, W. E. (1994). *A post-modern perspective on curriculum*. Teachers College Press.

Foucault, M. (1972). *The archaeology of knowledge & the discourse on language* (A. M. Sheridan Smith, Trans.). Pantheon Books. (Original work published 1969)

Freire, P. (1995). *Pedagogy of the oppressed* (M. Ramos, Trans.). Continuum. (Original work published 1970)

Gadamer, H. (2013). *Truth and method* (J. Weinsheimer & D. Marshall, Trans. rev.). Bloomsbury. (Original work published 1975)

Greene, M. (1988). *The dialectic of freedom*. Teachers College Press.

Greene, M. (1995). *Releasing the imagination: Essays on education, the arts, and social change*. Jossey-Bass.

Greene, M. (2001). Notes on aesthetic education. In M. Greene (Ed.), *Variations on a blue guitar: The Lincoln Center Institute lectures on aesthetic education* (pp. 7–43). Teachers College Press. (Original work published 1980)

Guillory, N. (2019). A love letter to black mothers. *JCT: Journal of Curriculum Theorizing, 34*(4), 1–10.

Hansen, D. (2008). Curriculum and the idea of a cosmopolitan inheritance. *Journal of Curriculum Studies, 40*(3), 289–312.

Haraway, D. (2016). *Staying with the trouble: Making kin in the chthulucene*. Duke University Press.

Heidegger, M. (1962). *Being and time* (J. Macquarrie & E. Robinson, Trans.). Harper & Row. (Original work published 1927)

Heidegger, M. (1971). *Poetry, language, thought* (A. Hofstadter, Trans.). HarperCollins.

Hillman, J. (1975). *Re-visioning psychology*. Harper & Row.

Hillman, J. (1996). *The soul's code: In search of character and calling*. Random House.

Hillman, J. (2006). Anima Mundi: Returning the soul to the world. In J. Hillman (Ed.), *City and soul* (pp. 27–49). Spring Publications.

Honorè, C. (2004). *In praise of slowness: Challenging the cult of speed*. HarperCollins.

Huebner, D. (1995). Education and spirituality. *JCT: An Interdisciplinary Journal of Curriculum Studies, 11*(2), 13–34.

Huebner, D. (1999). *The lure of the transcendent: Collected essays by Dwayne E. Huebner*. Lawrence Erlbaum.

Illich, I. (1998). *The cultivation of conspiracy*. Retrieved November 1, 2012, from www.davidtinnaple.com/illich

Jardine, D. (2014). Story-time lessons from a dog named Fideles. In J. Seidel & D. Jardine (Eds.), *Ecological pedagogy, Buddhist pedagogy, hermeneutic pedagogy: Experiments in a curriculum for miracles* (2nd ed., pp. 57–90). Peter Lang.

Jung, C. G. (1963). *Memories, dreams, reflections: The autobiography of C. G. Jung* (Rev. ed., R. Winston and C. Winston, Trans.). Pantheon.

Kauper, K., & Jacobs, M. (2019). The case for slow curriculum: Creative subversion and the curriculum mind: Resistive theories, practices, and actions. In C. Mullen (Ed.), *Creativity under duress in education?* (pp. 339–360). Springer.

Kliebard, H. M. (2004). *The struggle for the American curriculum* (3rd ed.). Routledge.

Knight, K. (2020). *The name of Mary: New advent.* www.newadvent.org/cathen/15464a.htm

Kovel, J. (1991). *History and spirit: An inquiry into the philosophy of liberation.* Beacon Press.

Lather, P. (2007). *Getting lost: Feminist efforts toward a double(d) science.* State University of New York.

Lindholm, J., & Szelényi, K. (2008). Faculty time stress: Correlates within and across academic disciplines. *Journal of Human Behaviour in the Social Environment, 17*(1/2), 19–40.

Martin, B. (1997). Teaching literature, changing cultures. *Publication of the Modern Language Association, 112*(1), 7–25.

Moore, T. (1992). *Care of the soul: A guide for cultivating depth and sacredness in everyday life.* HarperCollins.

Morris, M. (2001). *Curriculum and the Holocaust: Competing site of memory and representation.* Lawrence Erlbaum.

Morris, M. (2009). *On not being able to play: Scholars, musicians and the crisis of psyche.* Sense Publishers.

Mueller, L. (1996). *Alive together: New and selected poems.* Louisiana State University Press.

Myss, C. (2002). *Sacred contracts: Awakening your divine potential.* Three Rivers Press/Random House.

Neville, B. (2014). *Educating psyche: Imagination, emotion and the unconscious in learning.* David Lovell Publishing. (Original work published 1989)

Online Etymology Dictionary. (n.d.). *Mary.* www.etymonline.com/word/mary

Oxford English Dictionary (OED). (1989). (J. Simpson & E. Weiner, Eds., 2nd ed.). Clarendon Press.

Parkins, W., & Craig, G. (2006). *Slow living.* Berg.

Pinar, W. F. (1994). *Autobiography, politics and sexuality: Essays in curriculum theory, 1972–1992.* Peter Lang Publishing.

Pinar, W. F. (2006). *Race, religion and a curriculum of reparation: Teacher education for a multicultural society.* Peter Lang Publishing.

Pinar, W. F. (2009). *The worldliness of a cosmopolitan education: Passionate lives in public service.* Routledge.

Pinar, W. F. (2011). *The character of curriculum studies: Bildung, currere and the enduring question of the subject.* Palgrave Macmillan.

Pinar, W. F. (2012). *What is curriculum theory* (2nd ed.). Routledge.

Pinar, W. F., & Grumet, M. (2014). *Toward a poor curriculum* (3rd ed.). Educator's International Press. (Original work published 1976)

Quinn, M. (2007a). Desperately seeking psyche I: The lost soul of psychology and mental dis-order of education. In J. L. Kincheloe & R. A. Horn, Jr. (Eds.), *The Praeger handbook of education and psychology* (pp. 618–624). Greenwood Publishing.

Quinn, M. (2007b). Desperately seeking psyche II: Re-minding our selves, our societies, our psychologies, to educate with soul. In J. L. Kincheloe & R. A. Horn, Jr. (Eds.), *The Praeger handbook of education and psychology* (pp. 625–631). Greenwood Publishing.

Quinn, M. (2009). 'No room in the inn'? The question of hospitality in the post(partum)-labors of curriculum studies. In E. Malewski (Ed.), *A curriculum handbook: The next moment* (pp. 101–117). Routledge.

Quinn, M. (2011). On natality in our roots, routes, and relations: Reconceiving the "3 R's" at the rendezvous of education, citizenship, and globalization. *Teachers College Record, 113*(6), pp. 1214–1236.

Quinn, M. (2014, March 31). *New Orleans at dusk*. Unpublished manuscript.

Quinn, M. (2015). *Journal selection*. Unpublished manuscript.

Quinn, M. (2020). Between presence and absence: Living and learning grace in the face of death. In M. Bussey & C. Mozzini-Alister (Eds.), *Phenomenologies of grace: The body, embodiment and transformative futures* (pp. 85–106). Springer Nature/Palgrave Macmillan.

Radhakrishnan, R. (2008). *History, the human, and the world between*. Duke University Press.

Ransome, J. C. (1962). Bells for John Whiteside's daughter. In R. Ellman (Ed.), *The new Oxford book of American verse* (pp. 575–576). Oxford University Press.

Ravynstar, D. (2012, May 13). Goddess spirituality: Mary. *Journeying to the Goddess*. www.journeyingtothe goddess.wordpress.com/2012/05/13/goddess-mary

Rilke, R. M. (1993). *Letters to a young poet* (M. D. H. Norton, Trans.). W. W. Norton & Company. (Original work published 1934)

Salvio, P. (2007). *Ann Sexton: Teacher of weird abundance*. State University of New York Press.

Scott, A. (2007). *The nonlinear university: Chaos, emergence, life*. Springer.

Seidel, J. (2014). Some thoughts on teaching as contemplative practice. In J. Seidel & D. Jardine (Eds.), *Ecological pedagogy, Buddhist pedagogy, hermeneutic pedagogy: Experiments in a curriculum for miracles* (2nd ed., pp. 171–184). Peter Lang.

Seidel, J., Jardine, D., Bailey, D., Gray, H., Hector, M., Innes, J., Jones, C., Kowalchuk, T., Mal, N., Meredith, J., Molnar, C., Rilsttone, P., Savill, T., Sirup, K., Tait, L., Taylor, L., & Vaast, D. (2014). Echolocations. In J. Seidel & D. Jardine (Eds.), *Ecological pedagogy, Buddhist pedagogy, hermeneutic pedagogy: Experiments in a curriculum for miracles* (2nd ed., pp. 91–110). Peter Lang.

Spencer, H. (2015). *What knowledge is of most worth?* Palala Press/Alibris. (Original work published 1884)

Sumara, D. (1996). *Private readings in public: Schooling the literary imagination.* Peter Lang.

Taubman, P. (2009). *Teaching by numbers: Deconstructing the discourse of standards and accountability in education.* Routledge.

Trueit, D. (2005). Watercourses: From poetic to *poietic.* In W. Doll, J. Fleener, J. St. Julien, & D. Trueit (Eds.), *Chaos, complexity, curriculum and culture: A conversation* (pp. 77–100). Peter Lang.

Turco, L. (2004). *A sheaf of leaves: Literary memoirs.* Star Cloud Press.

Vaquer, M. E. (2016). *Poetics of curriculum, poetics of life: An exploration of poetry in the context of selves, schools, and society.* Sense Publishers.

Wang, H. (2004). *The call from the stranger on a journey home: Curriculum in a third space.* Peter Lang Publishing.

Wang, H. (2010). The temporality of currere, change, and teacher education. *Pedagogies: An International Journal, 5*(4), 275–285.

Wiggins, G., & McTighe, J. (2005). Backward design. In G. Wiggins & J. McTighe (Eds.), *Understanding by design* (2nd ed., pp. 13–35). ASCD.

Woods, R. (1966). *A treasury of the familiar.* Macmillan.

Woolf, V. (1957). *A room of one's own.* Harcourt Brace. (Original work published 1929)

Wright, R. (1966). *Black boy.* Perennial Library, Harper & Row. (Original work published 1937)

Yolen, J. (1988). *Favorite folktales from around the world.* Pantheon.

5 Complications and Threads

An Appreciation of My Commentators to *The Mythopoetics of Currere*

Mary Aswell Doll

I can trace the origins of my work to two events in my freshman year in college, the year I flunked two courses. The first event was a dream that foretold the death of my father. I think I dreamed it as he lay dying. I knew when I awoke that the nightmare was not "just" a dream but rather a foretelling. The setting, my father's study, was dark and empty except for his desk piled high with dentist bills, "dunned," as the dream said, by my brother. Duncan, my brother, had in fact been sending his dentist bills to Daddy. The dream's nightmarish lonely darkness and the uncanny word "dunned" so convinced me of its truth that I ran down the hall in terror and despair to our dorm resident's room. The two of us, Alice Johnson and I, drank several hefty tumblers of Scotch until the wee hours and I probably fell in love with her.

The second event was in a Shakespeare class the next semester. I was taking two requirements—botany and government (both of which I subsequently failed)—and a Shakespeare course (I passed with a C). Midterm grades revealed I was not doing well scholastically. With the death of my father, my roots had been severed. I felt I had no home place, although I was able to visit my brother with my mother during holidays. I found myself uninterested in food, like the famished souls of Beckett's work, and certainly was unable to concentrate. Dean Noyes called me in. "Oh," she exclaimed, "how wonderful to see you!" Then, looking at her list, she corrected herself: "Uh, oh, I'm sorry. Come in, Mary." To keep the scholarship that the college had set up for me, I was to go to the library every night, since obviously I was not studying. I did so. With my pack of cigs and a bag of books, I went straight to the smoking room and flipped pages. But. In that Shakespeare class, "Something" happened. Sitting in the back of the room, I stopped doodling when Mr. Seng asked us to comment on a passage from *Othello*. It was, I now remember from reaching back into the far past—some 60 years ago—a passage that mentioned the Pontic Sea. I have thought often about that passage because of its mesmerizing effect on me.

DOI: 10.4324/9781003231547-6

But what was it that caught my eye, or rather ear? for Mr. Seng had read the passage out loud. Somehow, that short in-class assignment so captured my attention that it has simmered in my memory's wellspring. I do not remember now what I focused on then, only that for the first time since my depression pulled me down, I had something other than regret and loneliness to dwell on and a sense, rather, that I could actually find meaning in literary texts.

These are the synchronicities—dream, text, and memory—that my commentators remark in my work. In those failing days I was not attending to the syllabi laid out for me, the clockwork demands of a program of study that excluded women (except, of course, for Emily Dickinson). I was a walking ghost: depressive and alone. But in another sense I was learning, as Beckett once said, to "fail better." My dream world ushered in a beckoning Something, the pull of inner life. And I acquired a listening ear.

In what follows, I weave the threads of my colleagues' ideas into the fabric of mine. Molly Quinn's writing style is animated, displaying montage, cross-connections, poetry, footnotes, memories, quotes: a web of ideas. Molly's is another kind of thinking, fluid rather than dry. Her thinking circles, is not linear, is livingness in sensual detail: specific, tasty. The creation of feminine consciousness, like Molly's, is the story of Psyche and Eros. But Eros is not the god of the moment; we still are hammered with hero myths. Dragons must be slayed, not propitiated, like the way our schools think the heroic student must meet the objectives, slay them. But stay a while with Molly. Feminine consciousness may be at risk in our grips by the patriarchy, but the empowering, engendering energy of Eros will lead to transformation.

Without Eros, teaching would be task-oriented, teacher-directed, and goal-specific. With Eros, teaching would follow a different pattern: tracks leading nowhere, mind awakening without fixing on any specific thing—altogether, in Keats' phrase, "negative capability" (Doll, 1995b, p. 52). This pattern, more a path, is not programmed to change the mind but to allow the mind to sojourn. Perhaps the mind goes backward—a good direction for rethinking, reformulating what others have instructed us to do, think. But the pause in our going is where we need to stop. Stop. Pause. Allow Something to come forward: "unexpected treasures and pleasures/to be found in a hidden flower-framed garden." These lines from Molly's opening poem express life's moments that yield mysteries—and for her, I suspect, a moment to recall her mother.

Molly writes extensively on slowness and stopping as modes of animation, suggesting various ways slowing down opens out awareness, she writes, to be "fully present together in the world." And that is Eros alive in our ventures. Molly's writing is knotty, complicated, conversant. Bill

Pinar's useful phrase "complicated conversation" is what makes curriculum both temporal and autobiographical. I think here of the song of the ancient Welsh bard: "I have been a drop in the air; I have been a shining star; I have been a word in a book; I have been a book in the beginning" (in Squire, 2001, p. 124). Thinking in the manner of the bard's "have beens" may be what Molly poetically calls "slow whiling," as in "butterfly effects."

I am grateful, as I think back through my life, of the "slow while" Peter Seng gave me in that Shakespeare class so long in my ago. And now, as I write during the pandemic, the virus has given us all opportunity to go slow so we can attend differently to what comes before our attention. Molly's many uses of the word "attention" is key to my work. I once gave a talk on the value of "attention" with similar words cradled inside, like "attending," "tending to," and "a tension." So I am compelled to return to my 1959 Shakespeare moment of the Pontic (Black) Sea passage (Shakespeare, 1622/2004, 3.3.454–459) so as to read with older eyes what I might have read with my younger eyes in the back of that room. What do I find there now? When Othello refers to *that* sea, is he referencing his Moorish roots, in northeastern Turkey—so different from the White culture he was bidden to in Venice? Did I think of that then? Probably not. But perhaps I did attend to the power of the sea's "icy current," cold and determined in its "compulsive course." My passive behavior might have silently marveled at the "violent pace" of Othello's mad determination, so different from my unconscious deliberations to fail. But pause I did, back then. Why do I remember that pause? Othello vows to "ne'er look back": Did that give me courage **not** to look back on my past secure life before my father's death but rather to move on? Doubtful. But Something caught my attention. Perhaps it was Othello's singleness of purpose that spoke to me, so disaffected I was then inside my sad self, so lacking in purpose, aim, or direction. And since I write, as Molly does, connecting time zones past with present, let me remark that the word "Pontic" in the Othello passage never once occurred to me until a flash back to memory only recently.

The depression I underwent in college was nothing like the depression my mother underwent in her twelfth year of marriage, when I was four. She simply could not fit in to the "niche" proscribed for her by the gender norms of the 1940s. She had what was described as a "nervous breakdown" and was sent to recover in Bloomingdale, an asylum that considered depression as a brain disorder best treated by electric shock therapy. So devastating was that treatment that my mother, later, put together a collection of fiction, from Kafka to Capote, that provided examples of the literary mind at work on "the world within," as my mother titled her collection (Aswell, 1947). My mother's world of the inner life, subsequently, I knew nothing about. We never shared our dreams, nor did we swap favorite novels. But then, I did not live in her literal house, just the house of her soul.

Molly's riff on her name, threaded with mine, in what she calls "autobiographical entanglements," opens out my focus on past sadness to present calm: Even in the time of Covid, we are connected. Molly tells us her name was originally Mary, which led her to construct a metaphoric quilt of Mary Shelley, Mary Magdalene, the Virgin Mary, all those British Mary Queens, tatted together with Mary Molly, Mary Louise Aswell, and Mary Aswell Doll. She shares a story about the funeral of her "beloved advisor" Bill Doll. To her surprise, she felt invited by Will and me into a family-only visitation before the ceremony of Bill's death. Will reminds me that, at that visitation, I said to Bill, "Good bye, old friend," a fond farewell to a decades-old relationship. Past connections are familial, yes. How difficult it must have been for you, Molly, the death of your beloved advisor, my former husband, whom I divorced. Perhaps you felt, as I did, that he was a father figure. Let me share a dream I had (January, 1994) of the confusion between father and husband that ultimately made me realize I needed to separate:

I am in a very small car sitting in the front between two people. The driver is my father, I am in the middle and the other person is an unnamed woman. We are all dressed in coats and I comment on what a tight squeeze this journey will be. My father drives slowly and keeps steering the car in the wrong lane into on-coming traffic. He does this absent-mindedly. Then he turns and we find ourselves in a recreation area—a large gym where a male exercise class is in session. My father now is Bill dressed in coat, tie, and slacks, attending his exercise class before we take off on our trip. I am annoyed at this delay and astonished that anyone would exercise in coat and tie.

The dream occurs exactly six months before the divorce, reminding me that I married Bill partly because he was a father figure. The unnamed woman in the front seat of that car could be an older version of me or it could be my mother (who wanted security for me above all else, urging me years ago to marry someone "noble," i.e., good with money). Something in my needs appealed to the "elder" or father aspect of Bill, whose middle name was Elder. I am struck by the pun in that last sentence that came unintentionally into my memory. Oddly enough, both my father and Bill were formal coat-and-tie kind of chaps, which my dream conveys. The spine of the dream is the phrase "tight squeeze"—implying, I think, that relationships should offer space, which mine did not. The dream's portrayal of the absent-minded driver is something father and husband shared, perhaps suggesting that they were not paying attention to the passenger's well-being. And the reference to coats? I dreamed in the autumn of my life.

Molly's piece resonates with me, as well, with her appreciation of stones, when she quotes me: "Memory more than memorization takes us back and down where our repressions sit like stones, the things and events that hold us down to a hardened literalism" (Doll, 2017a, p. 4). But, as I remind myself, creation stories from South America feature creation **from** stone:

> Raven stumbled over a stone which was hollow like a cup and he shouted at the stone. Karu, his father, told him to pick up the stone with which he had quarreled. Rairu did so and took the stone and put it on his head. It began to grow in all directions and to be very heavy, and Rairu said to his father, "This stone is very heavy." The stone grew more and more and Rairu could not walk any longer, but the stone still went on growing. It then took the shape of a cup which forms the sky and on it appeared the sun.
>
> (Von Franz, 1972, p. 66)

This is a creation-from-stone story. Indeed, sometimes the process of creating can feel very burdensome, like a great weight that hangs (in this case) literally over the head. But then, miraculously the stone changes shape becomes something else and creates a cosmos. Such is the power of writing, painting, dancing: creating. What is created is a new world to inhabit, to think about. In other words, creativity requires an interruption from outside the confines of ego consciousness, a smash-up. And what is revealed from under the rock is nothing less than a new world.

The stories of myth and fable, Molly reminds us, can be like Spider's box from an Ashanti folk tale. The tale is about a gold box containing all the stories of the world. Releasing stories into the world connects us, as Molly does, like the threads that web us together. No Pandora's box here! (although the name Pandora means "all gold"). How necessary to note the different "spin" between those two mythic female boxes (vaginas), one releasing all the stories in the world, the other releasing all the ills. Molly's erotic consciousness offers a rebuke to misogyny, so engrained in the Eurocentric imagination.

++++++

Even in the time of the pandemic—rupturing our norms—we can find portals that offer new awareness—"open spaces—for real intellectual curiosity" (Brubaker, 2016, p. x). Such is Marilyn Hillarious' suggestion as she shares her thinking about a more-than-human curriculum theory. Mythic fantasy is abundantly weird, but only if we forget the meanings of mythic images. When Yeats (1923/2000) wrote the line "Did she put on his knowledge with his power?" Yeats is suggesting an epochal event: Leda's rape by the god Zeus in the shape of a swan ushers in the ending of the mythical era with the birth of Helen and the fall of Troy. This rupture of the mythical world makes way for the Christian era—**minus animal power**. Alas! Mythical gods' interference in human affairs brings divine energy to breathe new life: the fusing of divine with mortal beings. But religious dogma prevents such thinking. Where myth has swan, Christianity has dove; where myth has bull, Christianity has lamb. These substitutions are deliberate, meant, I think, to lull the Christian believer into simple piety. Flannery O'Connor (1979) once said, "The thought of everyone lolling about in an emotionally satisfying faith is repugnant to me" (p. 100).

Myth, if anything, is a world shared with animal and godly power; is it a world of startling intercoursing. Such is Marilyn's focus when she discusses Richard Powers' (2018) *The Overstory*. To accept that there are other speakings and powers besides those of human beings is to accept a paradigm shift in consciousness toward Earth and Its beings. The wise ones who inhabited this Earth before us revered a cosmos that "spoke" in ways that are similar to the speakings of dreams. But, as Annie Dillard (1984) writes, "Now speech has perished from among lifeless things of Earth, and living things say very little to very few" (p. 70). Marilyn urges us to pause and drop into the portals that open out in front of us during this time of Covid-19 and its variants. Her commentary about *The Overstory* invites the reader to listen to the stillness the natural world offers us "as a vital means," she writes, "to engage in imaginative alterity with an external, historical, mostly obscure lifeworld." As Powers puts it, "A tree is a wondrous thing. . . . It even offers shade to the axmen who destroy it" (222). We should awaken to an ecological truth: This land is not "made" for you and me to do with as we please.

Privileging human life over all other life forms requires a radical shift in thought downward and backward: a readjustment of the place of the human in the larger ecological sphere. The problem is a very stubborn one. Marilyn reminds us that the Enlightenment's idea of The Great Chain of Being, with those two words "great" (suggesting power) and "chain" (suggesting intractable power), still holds sway and must be reconfigured. A downward/backward shift is a necessary blow to reason, "fueled" Marilyn observes, "by the desire to order, classify, explain, control, and predict." Exactly so. I have long been interested in knocking this formative belief off its cornerstone, which I had occasion to do in my graduation address to my son's schoolmates. Using the age-old formula for greeting an entire assemblage, I began: "Trustees, Administers, Faculty, Staff, Alumni, Parents, Siblings, Friends, Students, Animals, Plants, Stones: it is a great honor for me to speak at my son's graduation from his and my Alma Mater" (1995a, p. 92). The Great Chain implies other links, such as man over women, human over tree, two legs over four legs, policy over needs, and so forth. Readjusting hardened belief will require a shift in the placement of the human in the ecosphere. Why is this such a problem? Marilyn urges us as educators and consumers, as readers and voters, to appreciate the mysteries of the planet—deliberately using the word "mysteries"—by employing other nonpolitical approaches to climate crisis. She notes, with me, that the problem of our too-literal approach to ecological issues is not working. We must, she urges, imagine differently.

One way not to imagine differently about our ecological crisis is to read the teaching manual from the Center for Ecoliteracy. The manual states that to be "ecoliterate" is to acquire understanding of the ways nature sustains life. Herein lies the problem of policy, an approach that privileges humans over the environment, "life" as meaning life for humans. Students learn how to restore a watershed, how to feed nine billion people, and how to cultivate ecoliterate learning communities (Doll, 2021, p. 125). We are told that ecological intelligence benefits the well-being of humans and can be channeled to solve problems such as water scarcity, economic development, and population growth. All of this sounds noble, even hopeful. But the cornerstone has not been moved. People will benefit from these policy decisions, not earthworms or dandelions. As one Algonquin ecologist put it, "This sustainable development sounds to me like they just want to be able to keep on taking like they always have. . . . Our first thoughts are not 'What can we take?' but 'What can we give to Mother Earth?'" (Kimmerer, 2013, p. 190).

As well-meaning as the above project sounds, it emerges from the same paradigm of (White) People First. To think differently is to think sideways, to position the argument and its actors differently. Old beliefs, like old soldiers, never die, so we must help them fade away by employing different prepositions like "beside" and different speech modes, like hyperbole, exaggeration, and flamboyance, as in "camp." Susan Sontag (1964), the queen of "camp," has suggested that to reply to serious, rational problems with serious, rational analyses does not work in the present climate crisis. Working in the margins, beyond the pale, "queering" radicalizes thinking (Van Manen, 1997/2015). "Queering" involves undermining, unnaming, subverting. It works across disciplines, outside norms of gender and identity (Gough & Whitehouse, 2003). "Queering" seeks to destabilize established categories, particularly in the West, particularly about such chains of structure as hierarchy and power. The point of dualistic thinking is to straighten the problem by erasing wildness, uncertainty, performance, and chaos. The point of queer ecopedagogy is to think "beside" the problem.

And so, to add to the literary fictions that Marilyn introduces with the Richard Powers and Amitav Ghosh novels, I introduce Charlotte Perkins Gilman, who writes before this century and last, and offers a bedside (and "beside") setting for social critique. "The Yellow Wallpaper" (Gilman, 1892/2007) is narrated by a woman suffering from postpartum depression, deemed mentally ill by her doctor husband who prescribes isolation and bedrest as the cure (Doll, 2021, pp. 134–135). Readers understand not only the woman's intelligence but the author's critique of social codes governing marriage and depression. What logic is at work here? Clearly, not psyche-logic, since the medical treatment of the time is cruel. Describing the wallpaper, the woman relates: "I know a little of the principle of design, and I know this thing was not arranged on any laws of radiation, or alternation, or repetition, or symmetry, or anything else that I ever heard of" (p. 1396). This sentence alone demonstrates a revolutionary power of the unconscious imaginary, as articulated by French feminist theorist Helene Cixous (1976). The room in which the woman takes the rest cure is anything but calming. Instead of succumbing to her husband's command to be still and do nothing, the woman unthinks "the unifying, regulating history that homogenizes and channels forces, herding contradictions into a single battlefield" (Cixous, p. 881). Studying the wallpaper hour after hour, the woman begins to see another pattern emerging from the design on the wall. There can be other laws and other symmetries that form a pattern, not just the pattern of rest cure proscribed by her doctor husband. Nothing is really simple, she sees. Not all patterns must be linear. The woman's imaginary comes to identify with the wallpaper pattern, which adheres to an other "law" and ultimately frees her from the confines of the "pattern" of patriarchal command under which she had been held hostage.

Women writers have long queried the dominant discourses of their times: Think of Kate Chopin, Virginia Woolf, Jamaica Kincaid, Toni Morrison, Shirley Geok-lin Lim, Louise Erdrich, among others. I hope that Amitav Ghosh might agree that these named writers are not part of what he calls "The Great Derangement" precisely because their settings intrude upon consciousness, rather than the opposite, and by so doing present alternatives that defy established logics.

Our posthuman world where "humans are hybrids" echoes mythical stories and early wisdom traditions. The future may lie in the past reconsidered. James Hillman (1962), a post-archetypal scholar, suggests that the problem in Western thinking has been a disregard for mystical traditions, certain Native American cultures, and feminine consciousness, what he calls thinking with the left brain. He writes, "Of all theories of conception in antiquity, none persisted so through the millennia as the belief that the male arises from the right side of the body and the female from the left" (p. 235). The both/and rather than either/or shift in thinking reconciles opposites and privileges what the left (female) side controls: imagination, empathy, symbiosis, hybridity. Marilyn offers me the opportunity to extend what she appreciates as "an intense feminine consciousness" in the myth of Persephone and Demeter.

Persephone, recall, the daughter of Demeter, the upperworld goddess of grain and harvest and light, is in thrall to her strong mother. This is the mother who monitors the seasons, which she does in an upper-worldly way—in the light, literally in the spring and summer seasons. One day, out playing in the field, the daughter is raped by Hades, Demeter's brother, which so enrages Demeter at this rupture from her daughter and insult to her goddess powers that she causes the Earth to stop growing.

> She worked the magic of her terrible revenge. She made all fields unfruitful; she would allow no seed to rise out of the earth. Here was ultimate peril to all men and beasts. . . . For as men and animals could not live without plant growth, so the gods could not live without the sacrifices men offered up to them.
>
> (Thomas, 1995, *The Olympians*, p. 35)

To appease the Earth goddess, Zeus and Hades—Demeter's brothers—promise to restore Persephone to her mother, but only for part of the year. Hades, seeking the return of his bride, gave her a seed to eat before she left his realm. It is that seed, eaten by Persephone, that guarantees her return to the dark place. This is the seed of rebirth, the tie that connects daughter with mother, underearth to upperearth; it is the promise of the eternal return which Christians know in the Eucharist as eating "the body" of Christ. Robert Forte (2008) puts it this way: "The myth of Persephone's return to Demeter is a story about Earth on the verge of complete annihilation" (p. 7). Persephone's return from the dark is salvific because it is cyclical.

What is the pattern that would restore myth's feminine strengths? It is the pattern of a reconciliation between opposites: upperworld of light, underworld of darkness. Myth posits darkness as the womb to new life, new insights, just as gardeners know that planting seeds in the dark of Earth will blossom fruit and flower. Demeter's deadly response to Persephone's rape is mollified and reconfigured in the Eleusinian Mysteries. "The significance of the Eleusinian Mysteries is in its healing of a humanity afflicted by a one-sided, rational, materialistic world view . . . defined by the duality of creator/creation and with a religiosity estranged from Nature" (Hoffman, 2008, pp. 145–146). Myths tell their stories in metaphor. Most critics read this story as a metaphor for seasonal change. But we can read it even deeper as a metaphor for climate change. As James Hillman (1975) reminds us, the motif of darkness can be read as a necessary deepening of a too-whitened imagination of dualistic thinking. Resurrection stories, as old as they are, offer a pattern to reconfigure our climate crisis, since too few seem to care.

++++++++++

Brian Casemore tends to my work with the trope of "thread," tracing—tending—the various tendrils of my thinking in myth and literature. That apt trope includes work with students, who thread their own ideas into their projects, and the birth thread with my mother and then with my son. My appreciation of Brian tying my understandings with *currere* offers me a chance to ruminate in the manner of a runesmith, since he appreciates Odin's runic quest. The reference is to the sacrifice Odin offers to the Well of Memory at the base of the world tree—his right eye of literalism, so as to strengthen his left eye of intuition. To follow the threads of this tale is to delve down deep into the left side of Being that is feminine consciousness: of all that is non-literal, primal, fluid. I equate this realm, from which Persephone returns for a while, as the vague Someplace that beckons us in our dreams or taunts us in our nightmares. The threads that Brian appreciates go back to mythic origin, recalling not only my interest in Odin but also Theseus, who unravels the thread in the labyrinth that holds captive the monster Minotaur. If we cannot "name" what calls us, intrigues us, taunts us, shames us, we must follow the threads that connect our deepest beginnings and our release. Odin searching in the well of Memory, Theseus following the thread to the monster, are apt tropes for *currere*, the root form of curriculum, which beckons us to remember what we have forgotten, the primal Something that demands attention to our more-real self, waiting for a deepening. In his careful tracing of my literary interests, Brian introduces the shadows that taunt the positivistic assessment movement, with its insistence on clarity, goals, and objectives: tidy enough to fit into a curricular coffin.

Brian recalls my work on Samuel Beckett, which is infused with Something that draws, intrigues, torments his characters in a Between state of Being. Brian understands "something" as "the cryptic force or entity that ruptures literalism," a felicitous definition especially with the word "cryptic," as that which comes from the crypt, a yawning empty darkness. Two tramps wait; Godot never comes. Krapp waits to see if he can understand his earlier self, recorded on tape. He cannot. Winnie spends the duration of her waiting by telling herself stories, bits and pieces of the Demeter myth. Not only do these characters wait, they are psychically tied to an Other, be that an earlier self, an opposite self, or a mother/daughter pairing, recalling the Demeter myth. Beckett's characters are aware of—taunted by—a cryptic Being, to which they have access only in the stories they insist on telling. They are famished in their souls, near starving in the strangeness of their human condition; they are ghosts to themselves, off center, psychically removed from the core of their being begging to be re-born.

Beckett provides no release from that moment of immersion in strangeness; rather, he reminds us of its hold on imagination if we dare to loosen that hold, go deeper, recover the inner current, fail better. This condition of strangeness, so Beckettian, is like the Orphic doctrine, according to which the soul was believed to occupy a buried space within the body. It also connects (is threaded) with Plato's pun in *Gorgias*, 439A, that the body (*soma*) is a tomb (*sema)* in which we are buried. All of these references revolve around the idea of the doubled self, accessible only dimly. When asked by an actor what the pairings were meant to mean, Beckett reportedly replied, "It's all symbiosis." Translated, I think Beckett's dualities in various combinations revolve around the idea of being tied to an Other, be this other a younger self, a dead self, an opposite self, or a split self. *Waiting for Godot* displays this idea overtly, with two tramps (each other's opposite) and a master Pozzo, who is literally tied to his servant Lucky by a long rope. Whether we like it or not, all is symbiosis. Extending this idea to curriculum is Bill Pinar's idea of allegory, which has been a continuous thread in his thinking. By terming his method of *currere* "allegory," Bill brings together an understanding "of the connection humans have always had with other worldly forms" (Doll, 2017, p. 62). Part of this understanding of *currere* involves "recovery of the body, of feeling, of a primitive self which the abstract individual has suppressed but not escaped" (Pinar, 1994, p. 131).

Brian captures the essence of my work on Beckett with the essence of Bill Pinar's theory of *currere* with this wonderfully clear observation: "If following the thread of life exposes the tortuous path and chthonic complexity of a meaningful existence, it also transforms the practice of everyday life into world-making self-study." By identifying the place of otherness in my work on dream, myth, memory, and fiction, Brian calls attention to the significance of allegory as an essential doubling: back/forth, past/present, conscious/unconscious. And how is the two-ness accessed? By a beckoning Something, a primal Unnamable self, a truth of another kind, a primitive self. Something.

I first came across this idea of a Something in Richard Wright's memoir, *Black Boy* (1945/1993). He tells us of his encounter with "Once upon a time." Those magical four words ushered the young black boy into an undiscovered realm of his imagination. Never before had he experienced such a world as that portrayed in the grim tale of Bluebeard and his wives. "My imagination blazed," he writes. Before that, he had lived as a hungry child in the isolation born of a deprivation so profound that not even his mother could salve him. In point of fact, his mother tormented him, recognizing his rebellious spirit as dangerous in the days of Jim Crow, where even grown black men dissembled to be Uncle Toms to any White person— man, woman, child. Richard was too angry to pretend obeisance. He recognized "I was living in a culture, not a civilization" (p. 215). To try to teach him to be subservient, Richard's mother would beat him physically to subdue his rebellious spirit. But those physical torments, hard as they were, did nothing to deter the young boy from his fascination with "the forbidden and enchanting land" of words, spoken to him by a boarder in his mother's house. In recalling the spell that Bluebeard's tale had on him, he wrote:

> As her words fell upon my new ears, I endowed them with a reality that welled up from somewhere within me. . . . The tale made the world around me be, throb, live. . . . Reality changed, the look of things altered, and the world became peopled with magical presences. My sense of life deepened and the feel of things was different, somehow. Enchanted and enthralled. . . . My imagination blazed.
>
> (p. 45)

Brian identifies the place of otherness in my work on dream, myth, memory, and fiction. He reminds us that what is coiled and meandering in our unconscious can, as Wright put it, "deepen" the look of things. But this level of being, Brian reminds, has to be unfurled from the "thicket of experience." Brian's wonderfully suggestive word "thicket" implies just how difficult it is to recover the Self, so insistent are the "threads of difficulty" that lie below, beside, and beyond our conscious knowing. As he reminds us, a beckoning Something, a primal Unnamable self, a truth of another kind, meanders within. Recalling Madeleine Grumet's image of a lemniscate, or figure eight, Brian suggests the ongoing function of two-ness in human experience acts as "an infinite threading of alterities."

Doris Lessing (1975) speaks to this beckoning Something in her short story, "To Room Nineteen." The opening sentence offers the key issue: "This is a story, I suppose, about a failure in intelligence: the Rawlingses' marriage was grounded in intelligence" (p. 251). With this salvo against intelligence and sensibility, the story unfolds of Susan's growing unease with her ordered, gendered life, until she finds herself sitting in a big chair by the window in her bedroom. All it takes is one hour to experience Something beyond the window—a moment—that recalls the window scene in Kate Chopin's (1894/2006) "Story of an Hour," when the outside natural world sensed through a window brings immediate clarity to a waiting intelligence. In Susan Rawlings' case, the Something is a river in her garden that mocks her as a "slow-moving brown river" (Lessing, 1975, p. 264). Rivers are not supposed to be "brown," unless they are polluted. Curriculum theorists can attest to the central trope of Bill Pinar's theory—*currere*—the very root of the word "curriculum," which we understand as the current that flows within an ordered system. But in Susan's case, the flow is muddied, staunched. This is how I interpret Brian's word "thicket." Susan in the story understands what she is seeing in the river but sees no way to change her privileged life, which strangles her with its thickets of entanglements. Even the garden to which she turns for release is "thicketed" (p. 272) and her thinking is "wool gathered" (p. 279). All obfuscates her moments of being. Doris Lessing pays tribute to the feminists who had gone before her in her sly inclusion of others' key tropes, like Kate Chopin's Louise, like Virginia Woolf's Mrs. Ramsay, for whom the "cotton wool of daily life" (Woolf, 1976, p. 72) prevents introspection. I think Doris Lessing honors the feminists who wrote before her by slipping them indirectly into her text. Text on text builds context. Because these threads, to use Brian's useful trope, lead us ever deeper into our unconscious, they beckon our work as curriculum theorists.

+++++++

Finally, I appreciate the back and forthing of Bill Pinar's "Inscape," containing 31 footnotes in the back of his text referencing my *Mythopoetics* (Doll, 2017a). My reading his words was an active play between two spaces front and back of his text, like a performance, as in using the foot pedals of an organ in tandem with the keyboard, occasionally stopping to expand meaning. But just now I reread Bill's piece and realized that the physicality the footnotes produced requires a double flip: first flip from his text to the corresponding number in the back of his text, then flip to the noted page of my *Mythopoetics* book, next to me on a table. Text on text forms context. I think Bill's prepositional play of text on text beside text, below and back, again then again is the texture of *currere*. In poetry this move is allegory, Bill's named poetic term. All is double (sometimes treble). My three comments will follow the fugues that Bill orchestrates.

First is how the text of dreams offers images to understand the emergent self. This "coursing from within," when studied image by image and preposition by preposition, serves to clarify issues without. Bill refers to several of my dreams featuring strange images of my left eye. The dreams were "telling" me what I could not hear: the promptings from the unconscious to loosen my grip on normality—or rather, its grip on me. In three of my dreams, one almost after another, the dream featured a damaged left eye. At the time I was having difficulty understanding mythic stories of stones as organic, capable of movement and intention. My dreams were wildly insistent that I appreciate the beingness of stones. Imagine better! my dreams were urging. Think deeper! Nonsense, I kept thinking. Bill's reference of the wildness of unconscious images is precisely the dream intention to interrupt my stubborn wrong headedness. Bill cites Wittgenstein's ideal of a "primordial life, a wild life, striving to erupt in the open." Indeed so! Jung's understanding of the unconscious as primordial, a foreign being within, is very much akin to Wittgenstein, to Pinar here.

To domesticate the wild life is to hunt it down to the kill. I think here of the E. E. Cummings' (1963) poem "All in green went my love riding" ostensibly about a deer hunt. But Cummings puns on deer and dear, together with hart and heart, to rue wild life hunting as a civilized ceremony of death. The pageantry of a deer hunt, matched by the beauty of "the red rare deer," ends, after several stanzas, in something terrible: "the lean lithe deer" becomes "the fleet flown deer" becomes "the tall tense deer" and then the "hart" becomes the speaker's dead "heart." Game's up. Game's over. Wild life is dead. Bill's prefix "re," as in reconstructing, reconfiguring, regressing, recovering, acts as an insistent drumbeat to restore curriculum to its life roots back and down. To do otherwise is to "kill" the heart/hart that beats. Jung's (1954) critique of modern ways to educate was equally withering:

> It is ludicrous to say that the individual lives for society. "Society" is nothing more than a term, a concept, for the symbiosis of a group of human beings. A concept is not a carrier of life. The sole and natural carrier of life is the individual, and that is so throughout nature.
>
> (para. 224)

Another dream forefronts a key image of Bill's theory that, because we are "draped" with others' expectations, we need to unthink ancestral prohibitions and demands. The dream tells of being on a bus, where my grandmother reads me a letter from my brother. "I must tell you in all honesty" he writes her, "that I was very disappointed in the presents I received." I am annoyed. "What nerve," I think, "at his age to complain about presents!" The dream then shifts to a Christmas gathering at my grandmother's house, where she insists I wear her gown. It hangs from the shoulders in two long panels made from heavy, old-fashioned upholstery material. I don't want to wear it. "You can stand in for me at the party," my grandmother says. This dream perfectly illustrates Bill's idea of being "draped" by others' expectations for us, especially members of our own family. Ironically, I dreamed this at the very time my grandmother gave me several pairs of her shoes—a gesture, no doubt, she considered generous. Unlike my brother, I did not know how to refuse the gift. To wear the heavy expectations of our relatives is to feel "draped." Not to speak directly is to evade.

Second is the place of fiction for understanding the self. Early in his thinking about *currere*, Bill appreciated Virginia Woolf's novels (Pinar, 1973/1994), how "character" is made "expressive" therein. The one book I kept coming back to in my teaching years was Woolf's *To the Lighthouse*, itself an example of *currere* as the complicated conversation Woolf has with her characters, themes, and self. Mrs. Ramsay is Woolf's study of "character" in that novel. To her male quests, Mrs. Ramsay is all-polite, solicitous, saying one thing to soothe, thinking another thing to mock. Words echo but with different meanings, to suggest parallel realities of inner and outer life: "flounder" is both noun and verb; the word "fish" and the fairytale "The Fisherman and his Wife" play in and around the text in a sea of ideas, the novel itself situated on the Isle of Skye in Scotland surrounded by the Sea of the Hebrides. Mrs. Ramsay's knitting becomes Mrs. Woolf's knitting her mother (Mrs. Stephens) into a skein of ideas, knotty images, repetitions, "the cotton wool of daily life" (Woolf, 1976, p. 72). All this, so we do not assume "character" is a simple idea or that one's stream of consciousness can be dammed.

To the Lighthouse (1927/1955) was the text wherein Virginia Woolf would, as she wrote, "kill" the Edwardian notion of Woman as the "Angel in the House" (Woolf, 1942/2007, p. 27). Coventry Patmore's 1854 poem of that title paints an "ideal" of Woman as a superior, unreal being: "The most excellent of all/ the best half of creation's best. . . . For she's so simply, subtly sweet/ My deepest rapture does her wrong" (Patmore, 1854/2000, p. 1724). Such sentimental slop formed the gendered concept of Woman that Virginia's mother, Mrs. Stephens, believed like a religion. Her unconscious obeisance to the Angel code so fetishized her Being that Woolf's mother was silent about the sexual abuses Virginia endured.

To the Lighthouse is Virginia Woolf's revenge, demonstrating what happens when women, absent to themselves, allow men to run ramrod as guests in their house. The house of Mrs. Stephens' psychical self is the model for Woolf's portrait of Mrs. Ramsay's self and house. Both are falling apart. Mrs. Ramsay can make no sense of the "cotton wool" of her daily life. And her house is similarly uncared for: the greenhouse needs repair, the wallpaper is fading, the banquet dinner is burned. Just so, Mrs. Ramsay, as the painter Lily intuits, contains a "wedge-shaped core of darkness" (Woolf, 1927, p. 95). She lacks selfhood. A key moment in the text is the dinner scene, which seems "a single, bright, cultivated and civilized moment" (Greene, 1995, p. 98), featuring eight candle stoops down the entire length of the banquet table. But it is not. Each candle represents one of the Ramsay children on display, each one prey for the sexual intentions of the male houseguests during their extended summer stay each year. The portrait of Mrs. Ramsay, drawn from Woolf's ineffective mother, shows her turning a blind eye to the children's aggressive behaviors and the houseguests' stealth. When Mrs. Ramsay leaves the children's room at night, she leaves the door unlocked, letting "the tongue of the door slowly lengthen in the lock" (173). This loaded sentence is the gun Virginia Woolf aims to "kill" the ideal of the patriarchal mother, the Angel in the House, who privileges the sexual desires of her male houseguests over the lives of her children.

To the Lighthouse demonstrates what happens when the inner life is staunched, redirected from its powers to the constructed powers of the outer social world. As Bill has written, "Such a (repressed) self lacks access both to itself and to the world. Repressed, the self's capacity for intelligence, for informed action, even for simple functional competence is impaired"

(Pinar, 1993, p. 61). Mrs. Ramsay, locked inside "the cotton wool of daily life" is not "there" to herself or her children.

Third are family memories. In relating my work to *currere*, Bill includes the people he never met but knows of their influence on me, my mother and my brother. My mother left her children, my brother and me, when I was four. She did the unthinkable thing for a woman in the 1940s, but I am forever grateful that she did not do the unbearable thing. My earliest memory is of her leaving us. I might have intuited that her comings and goings in the house, the commute she took with my father into the city, meant that she might not return. This memory has the sense of my being "drawn" from my room to the darkened stairs. The stairs were directly in front of the front door, which, in the memory opened slowly into the dark threshold. "Is Mummy home?" I called down. My father did not answer, and I knew she was not there, she would not be coming home.

This memory tells me that I could sense my mother's unhappiness, but I felt "there" to heal her. I have no memories of her giving me a bath, reading stories to me, dressing me. But in sensing that she would be forever out of the house of my father, I sensed that she would be all right. I remember making her beautiful drawings to heal her while she was at Bloomingdale. We would wave to her from the driveway of the asylum and she, on the veranda, would wave back, slowly. I had no idea whatsoever that her absence from my father's house would be permanent, but I was content with the divorce arrangement of every other weekend visits to her in New York City. Consequently, my mother and I had an intermittent relationship (I never again lived in her house for any length of time) until her dying days, when I wrote this poem, imagining her as the speaker, with the I pronoun.

Communion

"My daughter writes poems."
There! I say it,
the fire burning pinon logs,
warmth in the womb of the wall,
my voice like confession.
I see you,
girl of my loins, daughter of my ribs,
cupping my words like wafers.
Take this, all of you.

We communed then, my mother and me, as never before. The longing I must have harbored for 50 years became finally a blessing, a communion. I suppose many of us have endured strange ironies along the way of our lives. Here is one: While my mother broke free from the cultural constraints against women, she must have felt that her choice to live openly as a gay woman could be too hard for me, should my lifestyle change. Change it did, but only after she had died.

My brother, too, in the 1950s, was tormented by his queer self, although he enjoyed lisping the part of Queen Elizabeth in a high school production, which I recall hearing my mother express her approval by her enormous, appreciative laughter from the audience. But. The pressures. The norms. The need to wear tweed. What finally broke the façade? For Mother, it was leaving the East Coast. For my brother, it was assuming a new identity and leaving academe. He was a good actor and knew the script laid out for him, but finally the pressure to be "normal" was so great that he simply disappeared into thin air. Just before his disappearance, I visited my brother in the locked rooms of the hospital treating him after his suicide attempt. (I awoke him from his deep, drug-induced sleep by holding on to the rings of the phone for 30, 40, 50 or more rings. I knew to hold on). This poem expresses my brother as cold stone before the warming of self-acceptance could enliven him:

Pygmalion's Reject

He was built a man before a boy,
a giant man built and bronzed in brain.
He lent his ears to accents heard beneath
the shelf of cloud around his head.
Are the accents there, we wondered,
so soft, so soft, and sweet
that none may hear them?

My brother, who named himself Bill Cutler, and who died of AIDS in the late 1980s, became a cultural icon, writing for Leftist magazines in Atlanta, being honored by Mayor Andy Young for his beautification project, and for living as an openly gay man with his Black partner. I miss my dead. Bill Pinar careful weaving of my mother and brother into the texture of his words brings them back and into the conversation. Thank you, Bill, for that and so much more.

++++++

The process of coming-into-myself could not have happened had it not been for my dreams and my work with *currere*. I taught myself to learn to loosen the hold generational expectations can have, can "drape" on us. Despite my stubborn insistence that all was right with my nice life, I was Psyche in search of Eros, which I found with Marla. Recall, when Psyche completes her final task of retrieving Proserpina's box from the Underworld (note! another mythic female box), she does what she is not supposed to do: she opens the box. At that very moment, Psyche falls into a deep sleep. Mythic sleep causes psychic change, a necessary beginning for awakening to the authentic self. Bill's introducing *currere* into the curriculum is essential to understand, with depth psychology, that Reason (and all the attending educational attributes called objectives, goals, and outcomes, along with all the attending social logics called norms) must be harnessed, always, in the service of psyche.

My commentators have not only interpreted my texts with skill and attention, they have allowed me to revisit the themes they discuss—memory, dream, myth, and fiction—which have been the loadstones that have guided my work. The work has been therapy for me, sussing out what shaped my obeisance to my patriarchal background. "Stay as sweet as you are" my Welsh stepmother would sing to me. Even my feminist mother, who left her children aged 8 and 4 to pursue her career as an editor, was patriarchal in her thinking about her girl child. When I told her that she was like Mrs. Bennett from *Pride and Prejudice*, seeking only to get her daughter married off, my mother was mock horrified. Methinks the lady did protest too much.

The stranglehold of others' ideas for how we should live our lives is a formative concept, which *currere* addresses. How can we get out from under those stifling expectations? Who is the Self waiting to be released from the demands of outworn social ideals? Writing has been my way of seeing patterns welling up from dreams and memory—the undertow of inner life—the inner coursing of character—so as to break free from their normative constraints. We can free ourselves from others' expectations if we dare to follow the threads of what calls us back to our selves; we can live the authentic, quirky life we were born to when we understand the forces holding us back. It is with gratitude and appreciation that I thank my commentators for their skillful and sensitive reworking of my texts.

References

Aswell, M. L. (1947). *The world within: Fiction illuminating the neuroses of our lives*. Whittlesey House.

Brubaker, R. (2016). *Gender and race in an age of unsettled identities*. Princeton University Press.

Chopin, K. (2006). The story of an hour. In P. Seyersted (Ed.), *The complete works of Kate Chopin* (pp. 1003–1032). Louisiana State University Press. (Original work published 1894)

Cixous, H. (1976). The laugh of the Medusa (K. Cohen & P. Cohen, Trans.). *Signs: Journal of Women in Culture and Society, 1*, 875–893.

Cummings, E. E. (1963). All in green went my love riding. In *E. E. Cummings: Complete Poems (1913–1962)* (p. 14). A Harvest/HBJ Book.

Dillard, A. (1984). *Teaching a stone to talk*. Picador.

Doll, M. A. (1995a). Dancing the circle: Cambridge School of Weston graduation address. In *To the lighthouse and back: Writings on teaching and living* (pp. 92–98). Peter Lang.

Doll, M. A. (1995b). Teaching as an erotic art. In *To the lighthouse and back: Writings on teaching and living* (pp. 42–52). Peter Lang.

Doll, M. A. (2017a). *The mythopoetics of currere: Memories, dreams, and literary texts as teaching avenues to self-study*. Routledge.

Doll, M. A. (Ed.). (2017b). *The reconceptualization of curriculum studies: A festschrift in honor of William F. Pinar*. Routledge.

Doll, M. A. (2021). Beside the point: Queering the body natural. In J. Russell (Ed.), *Queer ecopedagogies: Explorations in Nature, sexuality, and education* (pp. 123–138). Springer.

Forte, R. (2008). Preface. In *The road to Eleusis: Unveiling the secret of the Mysteries* (pp. 9–10). North Atlantic Books.

Gilman, C. P. (2007). The yellow wallpaper. In S. M. Gilbert & S. Gubar (Eds.), *The Norton anthology of literature by women: The traditions in English* (pp. 1392–1402). W. W. Norton & Company. (Original work published 1892)

Gough, A., & Whitehouse, H. (2003). The "nature" of environmental education. Research from a Feminist poststructuralist viewpoint. *Canadian Journal of Environmental Education, 8*(1), 31–43.

Greene, M. (1995). *Releasing the imagination: Essays on education, the arts, and social change*. Jossey-Bass.

Hillman, J. (1962). *The myth of analysis: Three essays on archetypal psychology*. Northwestern University Press.

Hillman, J. (1975). *Re-visioning psychology*. Harper & Row.

Hoffman, A. (2008). Afterword. In R. G. Wasson, A. Hofmann, & C. A. P. Ruck, *The road to Eleusis: Unveiling the secret of the Mysteries* (pp. 141–149). North Atlantic Books.

Jung, C. G. (1954). *Analytical psychology and education. Three lectures* (Vol. 17, R. F. C. Hull, Trans.). Princeton University Press.

Kimmerer, R. W. (2013). *Building sweetgrass*. Milkweed Editions.

Lessing, D. (1975). To room nineteen. In S. Cahill (Ed.), *Women & fiction: Short stories by and about women* (pp. 249–290). New American Library.

O'Connor, F. (1979). *The habit of being: Letters of Flannery O'Connor* (S. Fitzgerald, Ed.). Vintage.

Patmore, C. (2000). The angel in the house. In M. H. Abrams & S. Greenblatt (General Eds.), *The Norton anthology of English literature* (Vol. 2, pp. 1723–1724). W. W. Norton & Company. (Original work published 1854)

Pinar, W. F. (1993). Notes on understanding curriculum as a racial text. In C. McCarthy & W. Crichlow (Eds.), *Race, identity, and representation in education* (pp. 60–70). Routledge.

Pinar, W. F. (1994). Mr. Bennett and Mrs. Brown. In *Autobiography, politics and sexuality: Essays in curriculum theory, 1972–1992* (pp. 13–18). Peter Lang.

Powers, R. (2018). *The overstory.* W. W. Norton & Company.

Shakespeare, W. (2004). *Othello* (E. Pechter, Ed.). W. W. Norton & Company. (Original work published 1622)

Sontag, S. (1964). Notes on camp. In *Against interpretation and other essays* (pp. 275–292). Farrar, Straus and Giroux.

Squire, C. (2001). *Celtic myth and legend* (Rev. Ed.). The Career Press.

Thomas, G. (1995). Demeter. In J. H. Stroud (Ed.), *The Olympians* (pp. 29–42). The Dallas Institute Publications.

Van Manen, M. (2015). *Researching lived experience: Human science for active sensitive pedagogy* (2nd ed.). Routledge. (Original work published 1997)

Von Franz, M.-L. (1972). *Patterns of creativity mirrored in creation myths.* Spring Publications.

Woolf, V. (1955). *To the lighthouse.* Harcourt Brace Jovanovich. (Original work published 1927)

Woolf, V. (1976). *Moments of being.* Harcourt Brace Jovanovich.

Woolf, V. (2007). Professions for women. In M. Ford & J. Ford (Eds.), *Dreams and inward journeys* (pp. 29–32). Pearson. (Original work published 1942)

Wright, R. (1993). *Black boy (American Hunger): A record of childhood and youth.* HarperPerennial. (Original work published 1945)

Yeats, W. (2000). Leda and the swan. In M. H. Abrams & S. Greenblatt (General Eds.), *The Norton anthology of English literature* (Vol. 2, pp. 2110–2111). W. W. Norton & Company. (Original work published 1923)

Index

Adam, in Book of Genesis 24–25, 34
Albee, Edward 36–37, 41n20
allegory 27–28, 101, 103
"All in green went my love riding"
   (Cummings) 103–104
American identity 58, 62n5
Ananse (spider in Ashanti folklore) 81
"Angel in the House" (Patmore) 105
Antonioni, Michelangelo 34
Aoki, T. T. 36
Appiah, Kwame 25
Arendt, Hannah 51, 61n3
art 29n5, 33, 37–38, 41nn24–26, 71;
   art as experience 76, 84n14, 102;
   student artwork depicting Odin's
   journey 15–20
Art as Experience (Dewey) 76, 84n14
Ashanti folklore 81, 95
Aswell, Duncan (Bill Cutler) 35, 91,
   107
Aswell, Edward Campbell 36
Aswell, Mary Louise 35–36
attention 3, 34, 93
auras 33
autobiography: Doll's autobiographical
   narratives 6, 20–22, 51, 91–93;
   Jung's autobiography 11–12, 44, 70;
   and lived experience 14–15; Marilyn
   Hillarious's reading of *The Overstory*
   59–60; Molly Quinn's experiences
   69–70, 74, 79–80, 82; as rooted in
   humanities 19
Autobiography of Alice B. Toklas, The
   (Stein) 2
Awakening, The (Chopin) 36

Bataille, Georges 53
Beckett, Samuel 2, 9nn3–4, 28–29n3,
   92, 100–101
Beckett and Myth (Doll) 3–4
belief systems, chiseled 47
Benjamin, Walter 48
Berg, M. 77
"Beyond the Window: Dreams and
   Learning" (Doll) 2
bhabha, homi 25
Bible: biblical form in *The Overstory*
   53; Book of Ecclesiastes 36; Book of
   Genesis 24–25, 27, 34
Biesta, G. J. J. 51
Bildung 81
Black Boy (Wright) 101–102
Black Lives Matter movement 58
Blow Up (film) 34
Bolen, Jean Shinoda 57
Bollas, Christopher 52
Brokeback Mountain (film) 37
butterfly effects, in chaos theory 79–80,
   86n29, 93

capitalism 53, 59–60, 76
Capote, Truman 35
Casemore, Brian 58, 100–103
Center for Ecoliteracy 97
chaos theory 79–80, 86n29
Chopin, Kate 36, 98, 102–103
chronos. See time
chthonics 13–14, 21–22, 25, 29n9,
   83n1
Cixous, Helene 98
class inequities 46, 47, 59–60

.